C000220674

SPRITZ

SPRITZ

Italy's most iconic aperitivo cocktail, with recipes

BY TALIA BAIOCCHI & LESLIE PARISEAU

Photography by
Dylan + Jeni

Illustrations by
Matthew Allen

BANTAM PRESS

LONDON • TORONTO • SYDNEY • AUCKLAND • JOHANNESBURG

CONTENTS

DRINKS

INTRODUCTION

The Italian word *sprezzatura* doesn't have an English translation. Coined in the early sixteenth century by Renaissance author Baldassare Castiglione in his *Book of the Courtier* (1528), sprezzatura implied the sort of effortless grace that royal attendants of that gilded era embodied. For Castiglione, sprezzatura was a definitive pillar of true art—to work so hard at something that its beauty, to the beholder, appeared easy, agile, blithe. It was, in essence, the art of concealing art's design.

Today the word has taken on a more colloquial meaning. It's often tossed around in menswear publications in reference to details of rakish sophistication—imperfectly folded pocket squares, oxfords worn without socks, the perfect five o'clock stubble. Although the spritz and sprezzatura are not officially related, it's this I-woke-up-like-this mix of beauty and ease that perhaps best describes the drink.

This would, admittedly, be the perfect place to tell the story of our respective first spritzes, but neither of us can remember when we met the Technicolor dreamboat for the first time. It was likely during our "formative" drinking years, on one of a couple trips to Italy in the mid-2000s, wherein the spritz was likely shoved into an evening that very well could've included everything from red wine to lighter fluid (not really, but practically)—hence the foggy memory.

We do, however, remember when the drink became a part of our everyday routines, about three summers ago. Little did we know that this frivolous cocktail, seemingly built to be tossed back with abandon, had such a backstory.

While the proto-spritz can be traced back to Greek and Roman times, the modern spritz has its roots—the Italian mythos goes—in Habsburg-occupied northern Italy in the nineteenth century, when Austrian soldiers introduced the practice of adding a *spritz* (spray) of water to the region's wines, in an effort to make them more pleasing to their Riesling-weaned palates. The drink went through a number of iterations, first with the inclusion of soda water at the turn of the nineteenth century, then the addition of the all-important bitter element (which made it both undeniably Italian and a proper cocktail) in the 1920s and early 1930s, and finally the widespread addition of prosecco in the 1990s. Today, the spritz archetype is more or less a combination of three parts prosecco, two parts bitter liqueur, and one part soda. And thanks to Aperol, it's now Italy's most popular cocktail.

But more than just the ideal combination of bubbles and bitterness in a low-alcohol package, the spritz has become a window into understanding not only the evolution of Italian cocktail culture but also the importance of ritual and leisure to Italian identity.

Our homegrown cultural reference point for the spritz (or "spritzer," as ladies of a certain generation might refer to it) is a less enchanted one. It's a word that, for decades, was synonymous with perms, thong leotards, salad bars, and blush wine. Born as a half-hearted diet fad in the 1980s, the white wine spritzer was the softer sister of the vodka-soda—a monument to the era that oversaw the slow death of sophisticated flavours (and, simultaneously, many overwrought attempts at the opposite). But the current cocktail renaissance has left no stone unturned.

Now, in place of the spritzer, there are countless riffs on the bitter, bubbly, low-alcohol formula that has become nothing short of a phenomenon in Italy. The drink's blueprint has birthed an entire category of new drinks, from those that swap in lambrusco for

prosecco, tonic for soda water, sherry for white wine, and shrubs (vinegar-based fruit syrups) for fresh fruit. And though not always explicitly called spritzes, the low-alcohol cocktail movement, which includes classic *aperitivi* (drinks meant to open a meal, see page 14) like the Americano (page 99), coolers, and more, often carries spritzes under its own umbrellas of easygoing effervescence. Spritzes incognito, you might say.

With all of this avant-garde spritzing happening, we wondered what might be going on with the spritz in its spiritual home. How was it faring amidst the incredible success of the Aperol Spritz campaign, and what secrets did its stomping grounds in northern Italy still hold? It was out of a sense of duty that we went off to find the answers to these very important questions.

Over the course of ten days, we cut a path across northern Italy, from the many old *bacari* (wine bars) in Venice to the legendary Bar Basso in Milan to the old gilded cafés of Turin. In the process, we discovered that the spritz's biggest secret is that it really is much more than a recipe or a category of drinks that calls for the mixing of Italian booze and wine. The spritz is a regional perspective on the aperitif—or, as Leonardo Leuci, one of the owners of the Roman cocktail bar The Jerry Thomas Project and a leading expert on Italian cocktails, eloquently points out, "a cultural way that certain regions in the north—Veneto, Trentino, Friuli—think about aperitifs."

It's also a mantra, an attitude, and a state of being.

The spritz really is sprezzatura itself.

What we aim to offer you in the pages to follow is a glimpse of the spritz's past and present, in Italy and in the craft cocktail bar. We also hope to translate how the spritz became so much more than a recipe and a marketing campaign, but part of a ritual and a means to understand an entire country's philosophy on socializing—the "spritz life," if you will.

And after many a golden hour spent in the north of Italy, we wanted to extend and share the ritual back home, so we've provided you with all of the advice and tools to create your own aperitivo hour (Italian happy hour)—from building your go-to spritz bar to devising the ideal snack spread to match. We've created a framework of drink recipes that present the evolution of the spritz from classic to modern to the drink's philosophical relatives. But they are simply that: a set of little tried-and-true blueprints that are meant less as ending points than as trailheads.

So, without further ado: spritz on.

A SPRITZ IS BORN

IT ALL BEGAN WITH the Greeks and Romans, naturally.

Back in the fourth and fifth century B.C., when Alexander III was slaying his way to "Great" and Plato, Socrates, and Aristotle were fathering modern philosophy, these men were also, for all intents and purposes—proto-spritzing.

During the heady days of empire building, it was considered gauche to drink wine without first mixing it with water. "Only Dionysus, they believed, could drink unmixed wine without risk," writes Tom Standage in *A History of the World in 6 Glasses*. Drunkenness, as it were, was not next to godliness. Thus, lengthening and diluting the concentrated wines of the day meant that you could, say, drink a pitcher of wine at the symposium without getting yourself in trouble with the symposiarch (essentially an ancient mash-up of host and chaperone).

After Rome overtook Greece as the dominant Mediterranean powerhouse in the middle of the second century B.C., many of the cultural achievements of the Greeks lived long in Roman culture, not least among them the cultivation and appreciation of wine.

As the Italian peninsula established itself as the premier supplier of wine to the Mediterranean basin, a number of Greek wine-mixing rituals were improved upon, notably the addition of water to wine, or even seawater, as the Greek wines of Cos and Lesbos became famous for. Falernian, a white wine grown on the slopes of present-day Mount Massico near the border between Campania and Lazio, was considered the most expensive and sought-after wine in the Roman Empire, and one of the most mythologized in the history of wine. In a testament to the importance of the "proto-spritzing" ritual, even the oldest and most prized vintages of Falernian were mixed with water— an act akin to dumping your water glass into a decanter full of very old, and very expensive, Montrachet.

Bacchus wept.

While Falernian loomed large in the Roman psyche, a number of other wines established themselves as all the rage; most notable among them (at least for our purposes) was Setine. A spritz of sorts, Setine, or Setinum, was a strong, sweet wine often diluted with snow that became the premier summer drink and a pan-seasonal favourite of Augustus, owing both to its flavour (according to the Roman poet Martial, it tasted of salty Chian figs, for what it's worth) and the fact that it did not cause him indigestion. Other wines, like Mulsum, which had honey added to it; Conditum, which was mixed with herbs and spices; and Rosatum, which was flavoured with roses, were often consumed as aperitivi.

Fast forward 2,000 years, and the foundation of our modern notion of the aperitivo drink is being built, bar by bar, in northern Italy— first in the northwest with vermouth in the eighteenth century, bitter liqueurs in the nineteenth century, and a combination of vermouth and bitters at the beginning of the twentieth century (hello, Americano). At the same time, the northeast is busy with its own interpretation of the archetypal aperitivo cocktail: the spritz.

WATER INTO WINE

The word "spritz"—derived from the German *spritzen*, meaning "to spray"—is the first clue to the modern origins of the drink. The Italian legend is that the spritz either originated in the northeast of Italy in the nineteenth century, when the region was ruled by the Habsburgs (centuries-strong Austro-Hungarian imperialists who had some notorious trouble with inbreeding), or during World War I, when Austrian soldiers were, likewise, a fixture in the region.

These folks, used to their high-acid Rieslings and Grüners, apparently didn't take to the wines of the area, the story goes, which—depending on who you ask—were considered either too bitter, too strong, of poor quality, or all of the above. The Austrians ultimately resorted to ordering their wine with a spritz of water to dilute it, in an unintentional nod to the ancients.

As with most Italian tales of uncertain origin, the spritz story has acquired a very Italian dose of embellishment—including one dead-serious story a notable Italian bartender told us involving beach-going German counts and Valpolicella—to the point of parody. Roberto Pasini, in his book on the spritz phenomenon in Italy, *Guida allo Spritz*, sarcastically recounts an alternative origin story wherein a bartender, outraged at the notion that his patron would ask for water in his wine, punches him in the face, causing a "spritz" of blood from his busted nose to splash into his glass, colouring his drink a shade of red. "Okay, I allowed myself some licence," he jokes, "but I swear I based it on the most reliable historical hypotheses."

Whether or not the modern spritz's origins involve foreign soldiers with an aversion to the strength (or quality) of the wines is difficult to confirm—and every person really will give you a different answer. What we do know is that the early spritz was simply a combination of white wine and still water, à la Greek- and Roman-style.

But as far as we're concerned, even if the widespread practice of adding water to wine in the north of Italy—or at least the introduction of the word "spritz" to define it—does belong to the Habsburgs, the spritz really doesn't become the modern spritz until it gains its now-inseparable sparkle. Or as Guido Zarri, the former owner of Select (the Venetian red bitter brand often credited as the first to be added to the spritz formula), puts it, "the spritz is born when soda is born."

While soda water was present in Italy by the end of the nineteenth century—and siphons began appearing in aspirational advertisements for everything from Campari to Bitter Pastore in the first years of the twentieth century—according to Fulvio Piccinino, a drinks historian and the author of *La Miscelazione Futurista* (Futurist Mixology), it only started to become a widespread fixture in bars about a decade and a half into the twentieth century.

By the late 1910s, soda water was at least popular enough that it prompted the invention of what remains one of Italy's most important aperitivo cocktails: the Americano, which is documented for the first time in Ferruccio Mazzon's 1920 *Guida al Barman*. During this same time, the first iteration of the modern spritz began planting

1980S FLASHBACK:
THE WHITE WINE SPRITZER

The affluent eighties were all leg warmers, synthesizers, hair bands, and, of course, white wine spritzers. While the Iron Curtain was coming down and the stock market going up, the spritzer was conceived from the same health fads that birthed Jazzercise, the cabbage soup diet, and aspartame. Though not unlike those first Habsburgian spritzes consumed along the Italy-Austria border—simple, refreshing, and low-alcohol—the white wine spritzer had zero connection to European pre-dinner rituals, but rather, was born of the low-fat, "no pain, no gain" lifestyle. Fixed between manufactured wine coolers and boxed blush wine, this symbol of aging suburban femininity has seen a somewhat ironic resurgence amongst the cocktail set, which has banished all matronly implications from the modern notion of an American aperitivo.

its flag in the northeast of Italy and beyond. You could order the spritz *liscio* (plain) or spritz *bianco* (white)—a simple mixture of soda water and white wine that is now known as the "spritzer" in the United States, the United Kingdom and Austria, *gespritzer* or *schorle* in Germany, *fröccs* in Hungary, *gemist* in Croatia, and so on.

This white spritz, though, is neither a cocktail (the common creed is that a cocktail is not a cocktail if it contains less than three ingredients) nor exactly Italian. Those two designations come with the addition, in the 1920s and 1930s, of what is arguably the spritz's most important ingredient: bitter liqueur. When it comes to the modern Italian perspective on mixed drinks (and, sidebar, fascism—but never mind that), it's in this period that, according to Fulvio Piccinino, "everything is born."

THE RISE OF THE ITALIAN BITTER

The production of bitter liqueurs—wine- or spirit-based concoctions infused with bitter herbs, citrus, other ingredients, and sweeteners— and vermouth had become a cultural imperative in Turin by the middle of the nineteenth century (and earlier, in the case of vermouth).

Coffee, it turned out, was—then as it is now—inseparable from alcohol in Italy. By 1842 Turin had around one hundred coffeehouses, or cafés, that played host to a broad cross-section of society. Decked out in marble, gold, and glass, with preternatural lighting that seems to melt into the furnishings, the surviving cafés (many of them beautifully preserved) exude a sort of halo effect—as if to remove any doubt about their divinity within Italian culture. Manned by bow-tied and white-jacketed barmen, these cafés in their original forms may have been all-business in the front, but there was very often a party in the back.

The cellars and backrooms of these cafés became defacto labs manned by a *maître licoriste* or *specialiare*—an alcoholic alchemist of sorts tasked with, among other things, mixing formulas for bitters, both proprietary and from established recipes. It's here that some of the most important figures in the world of Italian drinks—notably Gaspare

APERITIVI 101

In simple terms, an aperitivo is a beverage meant to open a meal and is broken up into two main sub-categories: bitter liqueurs and aromatized wines. As a category, these liqueurs and wines tend to be mellower in flavour than their digestivo counterparts, or are served in a manner (with soda, mixed with wine) that counters their intensity.

BITTER APERITIVO LIQUEURS

This category includes all spirit-based bitters—typically coloured either red, orange or yellow—meant to be consumed before a meal. Generally those that are orange in colour (e.g. Aperol) are lower in alcohol, slightly sweeter, and less bitter, while the more ubiquitous red bitters (e.g. Campari) are generally higher in alcohol and more bitter.

AROMATIZED WINES

VERMOUTH • A fortified aromatized wine made by adding a neutral spirit to a low-alcohol wine, then infusing it with spices, roots, and herbs before bottling. European vermouths must contain one of three varieties of wormwood (*Artemisia absinthium*, *Artemisia pontica*, or *Artemisia maritime*) as the main bittering agent. While it comes in a number of styles—depending on geographical origin, base wine, and sweetness—the most iconic style is the original Italian sweet "rosso" vermouth, which originated in Turin in the late 18th century.

CHINATO / QUINQUINA WINE • Similar in style to sweet vermouth, but typified by the infusion of chinchona bark, or quinine, as the bittering agent.

AMERICANO • Similar in style to either bianco or sweet vermouth, but typified by the addition of gentian root (as well as wormwood) as the main bittering agent. By EU law, Americanos can be coloured either yellow or red, or not coloured at all (e.g. Cocchi Americano).

Campari (of Campari) and Alessandro Martini (of Martini & Rossi)—would get their starts.

While the café was a definably social place, the bitter liqueur was considered medicine, often sold based on your ailment. So how, then, did it go from being a cure-all to a symbol of Italian leisure?

"You had a lot of wine being made in the area, and by fortifying it or mixing it with spices and herbs and medicines, it was a whole other product that could be kept longer," says Rachel Black, an assistant professor of gastronomy at the University of Lyon who's done extensive research on Italian bitters, in reference to the production of everything from vermouth to chinato (aromatized quinquina wine). "So they created new products and then created a market for them through advertising." These advertising campaigns didn't seek to eradicate the medicinal aspect of bitters and vermouth (that still persists today) but to create an association between the products and a social moment—whether it's before the meal (in the case of vermouth and aperitivo liqueurs) or after a meal (in the case of amari).

Much of the imagery surrounding the branding of bitters not only featured your standard aspirational, upper-crust vignettes—couple at white-tablecloth restaurant in Edwardian garb, provocative lady sipping daintily from tiny glass—but also contained a "strong dose of forbidden fruit," writes Mark Spivak in *Iconic Spirits*. Bitter, after all, is a flavour that represents both poison and antidote (brassicas, anyone?). In one telling Campari ad from 1904 by Marcello Dudovich, the "bitter" appears to be represented by a slick proto-Zorro cloaked in all black, presumably seducing the woman sipping Campari at the bar.

Even Campari's current press kit plays up the sort of provocation evident in early ads from artists like Dudovich and Leonetto Cappiello, who is famous for his 1921 depiction of a jester climbing out of an orange peel: "With its colour, aroma and flavour, [Campari] has always been a symbol of passion. This passion expresses itself in terms of seduction, sensuality and transgression."

Transgression. We'll take two.

During the Futurist era (see page 17), the commingling of avant-garde contemporary art and iconic advertising artists like Fortunato Depero (who declared that "the art of the future will be largely advertising") helped further elevate many of these brands from mere medicinal tonics to symbols of Italianism—using imagery that seemed to suggest that, with one sip, sex, power, and freedom could be yours. With this in mind, bitters soon became more than a cure for indigestion shot back with the wince-and-bear-it enthusiasm of a dose of Robitussin. It was the core ingredient in a ritual—the text to this tiny budding religion called aperitivo—and one of the most important ingredients in a new Italian attraction: cocktails.

More than drinks, many of the first Italian cocktails—the modern bitter spritz, the Americano, and any number of Futurist cocktails, which adamantly called for the use of only Italian ingredients—were expressions of Italianness, regionality, and, in the case of the Futurist cocktails, an exploration of the contemporary Italian psyche.

Even the evolution of the white spritz to include Italian bitters was, in its own way, an expression of nationalism—an Italianization of a Germanic tradition inherited under imperialist rule. And it's in this moment, and the prosperous decades to follow after the war, that the spritz became a symbol of leisure and prosperity.

BITTER INTO WINE

By the 1920s, the social ritual of taking an aperitivo—whether Campari and soda, an Americano, or a spritz—had become big business in the north. Capitalizing on the trend, a rash of new products entered the market during this period—most notably, for our purposes, Aperol (1919) and Select (1920), both of which would go on to become the spritz's most popular bitter companions, along with Cappelletti Aperitivo Americano, aka "Specialino" (1909), Campari (1860), and Cynar (1950s).

Primo Franco, the third-generation owner of the famed prosecco producer Nino Franco, recalls that when he was growing up in the

THE COCKTAILS OF THE ITALIAN FUTURISTS

Just as the spritz was getting its legs in Northern Italy, Futurist mixology, an offshoot of the Italian Futurist art movement (1909 to 1944) was beginning to find a fervent following. Calling on ingredients both weird and ordinary—from anchovy-stuffed communion wafers to lambrusco to amari— the drinks of the Futurists were often less about ingredients and more about expectations—or rather, the unexpected.

Where the spritz nods to the past and revels in the present, the Futurists radically rejected nostalgia and were bolstered by the Industrial Revolution's devotion to speed, energy, and individuality. The art of time reflected that—praising achievement over harmony—often resulting in pieces that distorted perspective in an attempt to illustrate dynamism. Somewhat unexpectedly, the principles of the movement manifested in food and drink.

When applied to cocktails—or *polibibita*, as they called them— the element of surprise formed the basis of Futurist mixology. In keeping with the movement's mantra, the Futurists sought to reinvent the cocktail as not only modern, but as undeniably Italian, rejecting the use of classic garnishes and eschewing the use of foreign ingredients. But more than anything else—just like the spritz—the movement was about what the cocktail could inspire, socially and psychologically.

In the eyes of the Futurists, a drink was a temporary creation meant to evoke discussion, challenge expectations, and alter sexual desire and performance. For example, cocktails with eggs and spice were thought to lower inhibitions and were categorized as "war in bed," while "peace in bed" described digestif cocktails meant to warm those who were going home to sleep alone. Outside the bedroom, drinks containing sparkling wine (ahem, spritzes) were "inventive" and meant to inspire the drinker to create, while others were thought to help the drinker resist conformity. Once an all-but-forgotten piece of Italian drink history, Fulvio Piccinino's *Futurist Mixology* has not only brought the birth of Italian cocktail culture into relief, but helped explain why classic Italian drinks like the spritz were— and are—more than just drinks.

1960s and 1970s, the addition of a bitter liqueur to the classic white spritz was still "just a few drops," and was offered as a spritz upgrade. "You'd see a regular spritz on the menu and then a *spritz con l'amaro* at a higher price; it was the luxury version of the spritz," says Franco. Then it was merely a combination of still white wine, soda, and a dash of bitter—a far cry, says Franco, from the heavy dose that's now common in the spritz.

While Aperol looms large as the primary bitter liqueur used in the modern spritz, its dominance is a fairly recent phenomenon. Prior to the 1980s, when many of the bitters brands that once had a foothold in the market began to lose ground—from Rosso Antico to Gancia Americano—the spritz varied more widely from city to city, even from bar to bar, in northeast Italy. Today, some of these regional loyalties still persist. If you are in Venice your spritz will often be served with Select; in Padua it's Aperol; in Brescia it might be Cappelletti Aperitivo, and so on.

Just as there are a million tiny rituals in Italy, there are also a million tiny allegiances. "Which bitters do you prefer in the spritz?" is basically like asking, "Which soccer team is the best in Italy?" Even the precise manner in which the spritz is assembled (ice first, then prosecco, then bitters, and then soda) is not a joking matter.

Many point to Select, which was created by the Pilla company on the island of Murano (of blown-glass fame) just outside Venice in 1920, as the first bitter that found its way into the white spritz. In the 1920s and 1930s, Select ran a number of very successful ad campaigns—featuring famous Italian actors and actresses of the day claiming that it was the best aperitif in the world—that helped bolster its loyal foothold in Venice and surrounding cities. By the time Leonida Zarri, of the brandy producer Villa Zarri, purchased Pilla in the 1950s, Select was the company's most important brand, and the spritz con l'amaro—according to Guido Zarri, Leonida's grandson and the current head of Villa Zarri—was already an embedded fixture in Venetian bacari.

This spritz formula, a mixture of still white wine, soda, and a bitter liqueur, remains a consistent local ritual from Trieste to Brescia and beyond. But the spritz underwent one more important evolution in the 1990s, when prosecco—which by then was a market force in and outside Italy—began to replace still wine.

"The phenomenon of prosecco really happens at the end of the 1970s and the beginning of the 1980s," says producer Primo Franco, referring to the rise of the bubbly Italian wine as a global brand. Much of this had to do with the widespread introduction of the Charmat method—a means of creating sparkling wine by allowing it to undergo second fermentation in a tank rather than in the bottle, as in *méthode champenoise* or *méthode ancestrale*. This tank method generally produces wines of less complexity and longevity—but that was precisely the point.

"Prosecco became a lifestyle in the sense that it was an elegant wine, but a wine you can have every day," says Franco, referring to the sparkler's light flavour profile and affordability, especially in comparison to Champagne—hence its "poor man's Champagne" reputation.

With the advent of the tank method, the majority of the wines coming out of the region were sparkling (before this, Primo Franco estimates that half of the prosecco sold was still, or at least still by the time it reached the bar) and exported in greater quantities, carving out a bigger culture of sparkling wine consumption in Venice and surrounding cities, including the area's beach resorts.

It was here, on the beach, that the spritz met prosecco.

According to Vito Casoni, who spent twenty years as the marketing director for Aperol, prosecco and ice (the latter often absent from the spritz before this) became part of the spritz equation on the beaches and in the bars around Venice—notably Bar Capannina in Lido di Jesolo—in the mid-1990s. "They started to use a bigger glass to fit the ice cubes and replace still wine with prosecco," Casoni says. "The success of this was immediate." Seizing on the local popularity of this new version of the spritz, which was longer, colder, bubblier, and fancier (it was now routinely being served in a larger white wine glass rather than a rocks glass), Aperol focused its attention on marketing the brand via the spritz. And the rest, as they say, is history.

THE SPRITZ AS GLOBAL PHENOMENON

While the spritz had been the most popular aperitivo drink in the Veneto and many parts of Friuli and Alto Adige for decades, it's not until Aperol began marketing the spritz in the 1990s that it went from being a mostly local ritual to Italy's most popular cocktail.

"The spritz is not a global phenomenon," says Leonardo Leuci, one of the owners of Rome's lauded craft cocktail bar The Jerry Thomas Project. "Aperol Spritz is a global phenomenon."

When Aperol first began marketing the drink in the 1990s, the spritz made up "10 percent of the sales volume of Aperol," says Casoni. Today it is the primary way in which Aperol is consumed, worldwide.

By the late 1990s, Casoni began marketing the Aperol Spritz to other parts of Italy by traveling to bars from Florence to Rome and farther south, to teach the new prosecco-and-ice recipe. During this period, Italy was still dealing with the aftershocks of a 1980s countrywide campaign to curb alcohol consumption—and in a way the Aperol Spritz, at a maximum of 8 to 10 percent alcohol, was the perfect compromise. Between the late 1990s and the launch of the first Aperol Spritz campaign on Italian national television in 2007, sales of Aperol doubled.

The first ad campaign ran as a short spot with two women in a Fiat who get boxed into a small square filled with young people drinking spritzes; the bartender eyes the ladies and crowd-surfs two spritzes—made with soda, Aperol, and prosecco, of course—to them through their sunroof. "There was no sex or love story—just simple people," says Casoni. Just simple, good-looking people drinking in the town square during the day—no jobs, no responsibilities. Just spritz. It ends with a question, which carries far more significance now than it did then: "Spritz Life?"

"Yes," it turns out, was the universal answer.

Aperol's success in exporting the spritz all over Italy (and beyond) lies in the genius of translating the spritz culture of the north and the symbolism of the drink as a modern, tangible incarnation of the la dolce vita of the 1950s and 1960s—or, "as a symbol of wealth and prosperity of the urban people," says Roberto Pasini, author of *Guida allo Spritz*—to a new generation. "The lifestyle is simple," Pasini says, referring specifically to the culture of aperitivo and spritz in the Veneto. "Drink a lot, but drink well; don't hurry; and don't worry about your hangover—people around will understand you."

THE SPRITZ LIFE

ICE. PROSECCO. BITTERS. SODA. Olive. Orange slice. Clink, fizz, splash, fizz, splash. At 7:00 p.m., that is the sound of Italy.

A drink that hit its stride amidst The Italian Miracle, a period of economic growth following World War II, the modern spritz is something of a sociological oddity—a vestige of la dolce vita and the see-and-be-seen cosmopolitanism of midcentury aperitivo, exported with flagrant democracy to a new generation that knows nothing of economic miracles. The "spritz life," or #spritzlife as it were, is a "revision of that era," says Fabio Parasecoli, an associate professor of food studies at The New School.

La dolce vita if only for an hour.

The word aperitivo is derived from the Latin *aperire*, which means "to open." It refers, plainly, to the ritual of taking a drink—nowadays with snacks—to open one's stomach before a meal. It is Italy's take on happy hour. But it is also, as Roberto Bava, the managing director of Cocchi, points out, "an attitude"—a devil-may-care moment in the day when the Italian Dream (one not unlike America's, just with less working) seems a little more tangible.

If you stumble into any bacaro in Venice during the golden hours, or into Turin's Piazza San Carlo, or Milan's Navigli, you will find variations on the same scene—a sea of orange and red spilling out onto the street, clouds of cigarette smoke, and café tables littered with tiny plates of crostini, potato chips, and olives. How, we wondered, did everyone simultaneously agree to do this every day? To meet at the same place and drink the same drink, at the same time, like loyal employees clocking in just to hang out?

In the early spring, we made our way from the Veneto to Milan to Turin, along our own northern spritz crawl, four humans and their luggage crammed into a Fiat 500 like a version of *National Lampoon's Vacation* in which the Griswolds trade their Wagon Queen Family Truckster for a Little Tike's Cozy Coupe. All in the name of finding out.

Raised with the urban promise of never having to do one thing twice, we tend to regard routine as a synonym for resignation. But Italy is a country made up of a million tiny rituals that crisscross into a repeating pattern, which plays out like a never-ending run of a Broadway musical. By 8:00 a.m., it's the whistle of the espresso machine against the staccato of cups hitting saucers, a woman yelling something-or-other from a third-floor window as she pins sheets to a clothesline, while bicycle bells chirp like a gaggle of earlybirds announcing the day.

By 1:00 p.m., the ensemble emerges again. Waiters thread through outdoor tables, carrying steaming plates of pasta, the vibration of the customers' chatter punctuated by the swish of a wine bottle being pulled from an ice bucket. A thousand Lambrettas hum in the distance, providing the midday rhythm, until espresso cups meet saucers again and the masses retreat.

It'd be easy to write these scenes off as cliché if they weren't so pervasive in so many Italian cities. It's as if the whole country cast a vote on what its day should look like, asking only that it unfold with the kind of grace uncommon to two humans perpetually buffed out by the friction of New York.

In the fluid hustle and flow of the typical Italian day, there is arguably no time more triumphant than the golden hours, when the crowds emerge again, descending upon bars and squares in a crescendo that's a pack of tie-dye-and-denim-swaddled hippies away from the "Age of Aquarius" scene in *Hair*. They nibble on *tramezzini* (tiny crustless sandwiches, page 134) and crostini (page 144) topped with everything from figs and chicken livers to *baccalà mantecato* (page 151), spritz in hand, turning piazzas into their very own urban living rooms.

Describing Venice's St. Mark's Square in a 1938 article for *Corriere della Sera*'s monthly magazine, *La Lettura*, entitled "Omaggio All'Aperitivo" ("Tribute to the Aperitif"), the author might as well be describing a scene today, detailing passengers descending from *vaporetti* (water taxis), while sirens hiss and the "waiter lines up battery after battery of shimmering glasses." And for a moment, "everything on land and water seems to glimmer more than ever."

It's that glimmer that seems to live inside the spritz, like a snow globe that's trapped the life you'd really like to have. A life spent sitting out in tables lining the narrow canals in Venice's Canareggio neighbourhood as the sun gets drowsy and the waterways turn into glassy two-way mirrors, a life where the long-lost era of gilded Venetian prosperity is merely a partition away. It's practically a matter of ordinance that the spritz became the modern icon of aperitivo.

"Spritz Life?" asks Aperol at the end of its inaugural spritz campaign.

Who could say no?

APERITIVO TO THE PEOPLE

How far back the ritual of aperitivo goes really depends on how you define it. The Italians would be pleased about our invoking the Romans here, and it would not be false. The Romans did indeed have their own tradition of drinking wine flavoured with herbs and spices to alleviate indigestion or other ills. And by medieval times, the term *aperitivus* had come to refer to anything, food or drink, that had the effect of stimulating the appetite, often including certain plants that were either cooked or mulled into wine. They kept the ritual alive, albeit amidst excessive violence and the history's most devastating pandemic.

Not exactly la dolce vita, but still.

It was during the Renaissance that the first seeds of modern aperitivo were sown. Catherine de Médici, the Italian noblewoman who went on to marry King Henry II of France, was well known for her party-planning skills and, ultimately, her influence on French dining culture. When she arrived in the French court, she apparently brought her cooks, produce, tableware, manners, recipes, flair, and the social ritual of the pre-dinner drink with her. It was here that aperitivo became associated with the higher classes and typified by the ritual consumption of wine infused with herbs and sweetened primarily with honey.

But the social rite of Italian aperitivo as we know it today was born in the northwest as something of an urban manifestation of the rural

Piedmontese tradition of *merenda sinoira*—sometimes referred to simply as *merenda*, meaning "snack" in Piedmontese dialect—wherein workers coming out from a day in the fields would join their families and colleagues for a sunset snack usually consisting of various cold foods, like salami and cheese, served outside with wine. The tradition usually ran through the farming season, from spring to early autumn, and eventually spread to noblemen and women who would practise a similar ritual when visiting their countryside villas in the summer.

With the birth of vermouth—often credited as the original aperitivo drink—in the late eighteenth century, a culture of pre-dinner consumption began to grow up in the aromatized wine's hometown of Turin. But this was still largely a rite of the rich, as vermouth was, throughout much of the nineteenth century, considered *un vino bianco di lusso*, or a "luxury white wine," as Alfio Durso Pennisi's *Dizionario Enologico* (1910) describes it.

While it remained an upper-class affair, aperitivo had, by the early twentieth century, taken root in Milan, Genoa, Venice, and beyond. "From noon to one and nineteen to twenty it's practically impossible to cross [Milan's] Galleria without being seized by a friend eager to offer an aperitif," writes the author of that same 1938 article in *La Lettura*. By this time the cities had also developed their own respective aperitivo vibes—something that persists today. Milan's Galleria was "ecumenical and bourgeois," Rome's Via Veneto had "an easy spirit," while Turin's scene—housed beneath the city's famous *portici*, or classical porticos—was "dignified and chatty." If you really wanted to get the full effect of aperitivo, you had to head to Venice's St. Mark's Square, where "even the pigeons, it seems, are enchanting."

In the years following the World War II—once Mussolini's fascist government had been overthrown and Italy entered that famous period of economic growth—aperitivo became the collective, democratic social ritual it is today. The dream of Italy that took form in those Turinese coffeehouses during the middle-to-late nineteenth century of a unified, prosperous Italy had finally taken hold. It's this era that bore the cultural kaleidoscope through which we still view Italy—all Lambrettas and Vespas, white linen, and Portofino; the Italy of Fellini and the era of "Hollywood on the Tiber." This vision of the country is still exported (even to Italians) with the same tinge of exoticism reserved for tiki culture or the samba. And in a way, it's this same vision of Italy that was repackaged for a new generation of drinkers in the 1990s.

THE SPRITZ TRAIL

Venice, it turns out, had no use for our tiny Fiat coupe. This is a walking city, and it's a good thing, because there is a real reason why the Venetians are regarded as some of Italy's most enthusiastic drinkers: they can drink.

Around two hundred and sixty thousand people call the Floating City home, while an estimated twenty-two million pass through it each year. But despite the odds, the spritz life still feels most deeply ingrained, and best preserved in its true form, here. There are very few *apericena* buffets (the much-maligned mutation of aperitivo into *cena*, or dinner, featuring mostly cheap, low-quality food) and almost no overwrought cocktails outside the hotels; even updates on classic *cicchetti* (small bites, mean to be consumed at a bar) hew closely to, or riff off of, traditional Venetian recipes. And while food is not included in the price of your drink, as it generally is in Turin and Milan, a spritz will run you around three euros and accompanying cicchetti rarely crest over a euro or two.

Aperitivo hour is arguably at its finest in Canareggio—which feels a world away from St. Mark's selfie sticks and packs of German tourists dressed as if ready, at any moment, to scale a cliff. As the sun began to set, we piled into any number of bacari, like Al Timon—a kinetic little spot that makes its bones during the golden hours serving plates piled high with crostini anointed with toppings like smoked mozzarella and tomatoes, baccalà mantecato, and chicken livers, all of it washed down with spritz al bitter after spritz al bitter. And then it's on to the next one.

Like the tapas tradition in Spain—moving from bar to bar sampling a few small bites at each—aperitivo in Venice is best experienced as a moveable (mostly liquid) feast. Or, as the Venetians call it, *giro di ombre*, which refers both to a round of drinks (*ombre* is a dialectical

THE SPRITZ TRAIL

MILAN

BRESCIA

TURIN

TRENTO

TRIESTE

VENICE

PADUA

word for glass of wine or drink) and the act of taking aperitivo in rounds—spreading it between a couple of bacari and letting it last as long as you can stand. (Tradition dictates that if you want to make it to dinner, you best limit the number of people you're rolling with—each person in your group counts as one round.)

"[In Venice], teetotallers have great social problems," says Michela Scibila, a Venice native and the author of a number of guides to the city's wine bars and restaurants. No joke. We quickly acquired the hangovers to prove it.

From Venice and on through the spritz's other two Veneto strongholds—Treviso (capital of prosecco) and Padua (home of Aperol)—you'll find the same talent for drinking and a similar passion for aperitivo.

These surrounding regions hew relatively closely to Venetian tradition, with a few departures. In Padua, for example, you'll often find slight variations of the spritz that include everything from Aperol to Cynar to Campari to Select to gin. Some even go so far as to assert that a true Paduan spritz features a combination of all five (god help those people).

Further north along the spritz trail, the variation that used to be much more common before the spritz became synonymous with Aperol still persists. Amidst the Dolomites, in Alto Adige, the spritz even loses its bitter altogether, subbing in *acqua santa* (holy water), which refers to an elderflower cordial that's often made locally by allowing the flowers and sugar to ferment in the sun. It's used in the Hugo Spritz (page 81)—a simple mixture of elderflower syrup, mint, prosecco, and soda, garnished with a lemon—the second most popular spritz behind the classic Venetian formula.

Down from the mountains and through Brescia, the locals call their spritz *pirlo*, which, in the Brescian dialect, means "fall," referring to the way the red bitter descends through the drink and to the bottom of the glass. Brescia is a Lombardian town just west of Lake Garda and about an hour by car from Milan, where Cappelletti's red bitter—which originated just after World War I and is commonly referred to in the area as Specialino—has maintained a stronghold. It's typically consumed

with white wine and soda as a variation on the Bicicletta (page 62)—
a popular Campari-based Milanese version of the spritz invented in
the 1930s.

It's in Milan that the pre-dinner scene shifts drastically. We had our first
Milanese spritz at Armani Café (yes, that Armani), a half-serious stop
on our planned route, where you'll find your reflection in every surface
and no shortage of studded and bedazzled attire.

We wouldn't dare judge Milan from this vantage point, but as a
cosmopolitan town that's provided the industrial heartbeat of Italy
for decades, there's no denying that it's a severe, hulking city in
comparison to Venice and its environs. But it's true that beneath the
facade there is more energy for the new than anywhere else in Italy—
which is why aperitivo has strayed so far from tradition here, both in
form and purpose.

"Milano is really the only city in Italy where aperitivo is a mix of
pleasure and business at the same time," says Maurizio Stocchetto,
the owner of Bar Basso, one of Milan's most famous and traditional
bars and the birthplace of the Negroni's bubbly cousin, the Negroni
Sbagliato (page 58).

All mirrors and gold, emerald velvet, and vintage glassware, Bar Basso
had us rubbing elbows with marketing men in suits, women who looked
like they'd rolled out of a Dolce & Gabbana display window, old men,
tourists, and a few sophisticated university students.

The bar swells, starting around 6:30 p.m., to two- or three-deep, a
cabinet full of crostini and tramezzini are discharged to the tables and
bar tops with rapid fire, while Negronis and their Sbagliato siblings are
served in handblown goblets the size of pineapples.

Beyond legendary bars like Bar Basso and Caffé Camparino (a
glittering art nouveau bar in the Galleria), Milan's aperitivo trail twists
and turns through spots serving everything from sushi to crudité, from
spritzes and sbagliatos to craft cocktails that could've been plucked
from any number of urban menus. Milan is the only city where that
pattern of tiny rituals is constantly being unravelled, and then ravelled
again.

But less than two hours away to the west, the clock seems determined to stop. Turin is a city that is as notorious for its stuck-in-time nature as Venice is for hitting the bottle. The capital of coffee and chocolate, and the former seat of the Savoy Kingdom, it feels more like a French city—hence its "little Paris" nickname—than an Italian one, with its baroque architecture, grand portico–encased walkways, and wide boulevards.

Culturally, it's just as baroque. Its people are regarded as being among Italy's most traditional, many of them taking their aperitivo in the same grandiose bars—Caffé Mulassano, Caffé Turin, Caffé San Carlo—that Turin residents frequented a century ago. And in a manner so dignified that it feels downright anti-modern.

Fittingly, of all the northern Italian cities, there is no place where aperitivo is quite as grand. While Turin isn't immune to the budget apericena deluge of soggy *pizzetta* and yesterday's pasta, it's here that a more buttoned-up sort of buffet spread has its longest history. Tiered platters piled with tiny *stuzzichini*, or "finger foods," coiffed Turinese bathed in yellow light sipping spritz and vermouth—it's a scene that likely would have made Catherine de Médici proud. "Under the portici," the scene, it turns out, is indeed, "dignified and chatty." And it's fitting to have put our coupe to rest under those portici, where the ritual of aperitivo that bore the modern spritz began.

So, you might ask, all of this running around for just one drink? But who wouldn't want to chase the drink that symbolizes, for much of Italy, that all-important transition from work to play?

It's a drink splashed together with a rakish dedication to leisure, and one served during a sacred time of day that asks nothing except, says Roberto Bava of Cocchi, "that you be yourself." And after one or two—like a beloved friend or trusted companion—the spritz's bewitching plea to pause and drink draws out the best in all of us. Because who *isn't* better, and perhaps more oneself, with a spritz in hand?

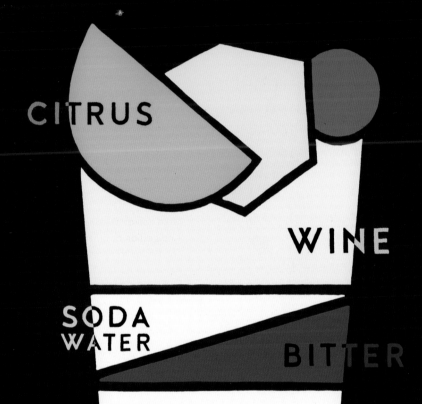

CITRUS

WINE

SODA
WATER

BITTER

SPRITZ COCKTAILS

IN VENICE, THE SPIRITUAL home of the spritz, there are no house-conceived twists on the old-fashioned, curious margaritas, or midori-infused variations on the martini (unless you happen to be at a hotel or an establishment with a doorman and electronic dance music spilling out from inside, in which case: avoid). Instead, there is simply an assembly line of prosecco, soda water, and bitter liqueurs combined by the slapdash dozen with a spraying soda gun and speed pourer. And your drink is always, without fail, punctuated with a skewered olive or a slice of orange plunging to the bottom with a bubbling plunk. Serious only in its insistent daily presence, the purest spritz is made by feel, gut instinct, and experimentation. Yet, in order to offer insight into its evolution and architecture—no matter how resistant to the jigger— there must be a set of rules for building it.

HOW TO SPRITZ

FIRST • A spritz is always effervescent. Whether its bubble is acquired through soda water, prosecco, some other sparkling wine, or a flavoured soda, the spritz would not be a spritz without buoyancy.

SECOND • A spritz is low in alcohol, which, for our purposes, means that it should contain no more than one ounce of strong spirits (preferably less). This is a drink that is consumed when the day is waning and the night is young.

THIRD • A spritz is a pre-dinner drink, meant to be consumed in that liminal hour between work and play. It should be bitter as a means to open the stomach for a meal.

Within this chapter, we offer models that follow the aforementioned rules, from classic to modern to a smattering of oddball cousins and back again. We remind you, of course, that these are simply jumping-off points for creating a spritz. If an ingredient is absent from your bar, try a substitute—Cocchi Americano for bianco vermouth, lime juice for lemon juice, or tonic water for quinquina wine, and so on—because the true spirit of the spritz requires a bit of homegrown curiosity for what might happen if you stretch the rules just a little bit.

PROSECCO 101

Prosecco is oft-maligned as being the ubiquitous, cheap cousin of Champagne—the kind of sparkling wine that's fuelled many a bottomless brunch. It's true that a deluge of cheap prosecco began cascading into the United States and United Kingdom in the 1980s and into the 1990s, when restaurants began pouring the stuff directly into the mouths of celebrities and the linen-clad set. It's since become something of a global lifestyle brand, much of this owed to its production process, called the Charmat method—a means of creating sparkling wine by allowing it to undergo its second fermentation in a tank rather than in the bottle, which is the way true Champagne is made. This tank method, which is much less time-consuming and more affordable, generally produces wines of less complexity and longevity, which is precisely why prosecco ended up in nightclubs, bars, and pretty much every place alcohol is served from New York to Hong Kong. But the wines do have a more serious side.

The finest proseccos come from the DOCG zone, which stretches from the town of Conegliano to Valdobbiadene, and covers fifty thousand acres of steep, terraced vineyards that rise up from the road like verdant amphitheatres. While the majority of the region's sparkling wines—all produced from the white Glera grape—are made using the Charmat method, the last half decade has seen a very welcome redux of prosecco *col fondo* (which translates to "with its bottom" or "with its sediment"), the old-school cloudy style of bottle-fermented bubbly that's released without the lees being removed. While not a typical companion for the spritz, the col fondo style has captured the attention of the wine world's avant-garde as a more traditional, and very often more compelling, expression of the region.

SPRITZ GO-TOS

When spritzing, you'll typically want to look for a dry prosecco made using the Charmat method; those clean, bright pear notes and sheer slammability are paramount here. So is quality. Just because you're mixing doesn't mean you can get away with a suspect bottle of bubbly. In many of the classic and modern spritz formulas, prosecco makes up the majority of the drink, and—plain and simple—the better the prosecco, the better the drink. Below are three producers who make top-quality Charmat-method prosecco.

NINO FRANCO • For three generations the Franco family has been making some of the best prosecco out there. While the single-cru bottlings are worth seeking out on their own, the Rustico bottling is our favourite all-purpose prosecco and clocks in at just £18 per bottle.

SORELLE BRONCA • The sisters Bronca are some of the region's most conscientious growers and producers. They tend organically-farmed hillside vineyards in Conegliano, which feeds their range of proseccos. At the top end is one of the region's best Charmat wines, Particella 68, along with a limited col fondo bottling. For our everyday purposes both the Extra Dry (£18) and the Brut (£18), which, confusingly enough, has a touch more residual sugar than the Extra Dry, are both excellent.

ADAMI • Like Nino Franco, Adami produces a significant volume of prosecco, but the quality level remains very high. Known at the top end for their Vigneto Giardino bottling, they also offer the affordable Garbèl (£15) and Bosco di Gica (£16), which both play nice in any spritz.

COL FONDO

Some of the most exciting wines in the region are being made in this style. Here are a few worth seeking out:

Casa Coste Piane Prosecco Valdobbiadene "Sur Lie" NV | £17
Ca dei Zago Col Fondo Prosecco NV | £19
Bele Casel Col Fondo Prosecco Asolo DOCG NV | £17
Zanotto Col Fondo Prosecco NV | £18

SPRITZ STYLES

Throughout the recipe section we've categorized spritzes as either Classic, Modern, or Cousins.

Classic

The most traditional spritzes are those that originate along Italy's spritz trail—from Trieste to Turin. They're the simplest of the formulas, containing just a few ingredients: wine or prosecco, soda water, a bit of citrus, and a bitter element like Aperol, Campari, or in some cases, an amaro like Cynar. The classic spritzes evolved regionally and are topped with a distinguishing garnish; their bitters are determined by a particular allegiance to one local brand or another. All of the spritzes that make up the classic canon—from the Venetian Spritz to the Negroni Sbagliato—are still drunk in their respective homes, like a daily prayer to the aperitivo gods.

Modern

Once the Italian version of the spritz hit the U.S., the U.K. and beyond, bartenders took note and began mixing their own versions of the iconic cocktail. These modern drinks still adhere closely to the classic template for the spritz but they prove that there are dozens of possible combinations within that format, especially when bred with classic cocktails whose spirit base can be swapped out for sparkling wine. The modern spritz takes cues from its predecessors but draws on new garnishes, fresh juices, and alternatives to the classic Italian liqueurs that commonly find their way into the spritz.

Cousins

The cousins of the spritz are so called because they aren't necessarily made up of the exact same DNA. While they maintain the same philosophical sensibilities (bitter, low-alcohol, bubbly), they do so with unorthodox ingredients (egg whites, beer, muddled fruit) that pull them off the beaten path. Spritzes in camouflage, they share the same ethos as a classic or modern iteration.

BUILDING A SPRITZ BAR

The essential spritz bar is a spare one, requiring only the elements detailed in "How to Spritz" (page 38)—namely, something bubbly and something bitter, with a wine base, which can be anything from still white wine to prosecco to vermouth to sherry. Beyond the essentials, there are a number of highly recommended additions—from syrups to shrubs to a greater selection of liqueurs—that can easily add another layer of complexity to the spritz.

But even if you haven't begun to acquire these ingredients, you probably have the makings of a spritz to hand. Given the up-for-anything nature of the drink, anything on one's bar—Angostura bitters to Barolo Chinato—is fair game. But take heed: not all experiments will result in deliciousness, we can assure you of that. Though it invites experimentation, the spritz requires a feel for flavour pairing and the necessary grace to understand that sometimes less is more. Often, the simplest spritzes are the most alluring.

Following is a brief list of recommended necessities with suggestions for the advanced home bar or bartender.

Bubbles

SODA WATER • The Soda Stream is your best bet to ensure an endless supply of charged soda water. Newer models allow for the user to gauge the level of carbonation, and the spritz is always best at its most bubbly. In terms of store-bought soda water, Canada Dry's aggressive carbonation is a great baseline, but any carbonated water will do.

SPARKLING WINE • While prosecco (see page 40) is the spritz's bubbly best friend, any sparkling wine is fair game. For a spritz that has the bulk and structure to stand up to cold weather, look to lambrusco. If you're seeking an extra layer of complexity from your bubbly wine—especially when pairing with minimal ingredients that allow the wine to shine—Crémant d'Alsace, which is an affordable alternative to Champagne and is made in the same method, will add a note of yeasty umami flavor.

TONIC WATER • Our go-to is always Fever Tree, which is notable for its subtle spice, dry finish, and ability to play well with other ingredients. Tonic syrups, like Jack Rudy or Tomr's, are also quite versatile, but they will most

likely include more intense herbal and spice flavours, so try them out in small amounts before committing to a generous dose. Also, keep in mind that most commercial tonic waters lean towards sweet and overpowering, so if Schweppes is all you've got to hand, be prepared to use less tonic and to supplement with soda water.

Bitter Aperitivo Liqueurs and Wines

For more on aperitivi, turn to the "Aperitivi 101" box on page 14.

CAMPARI • In 1860, Gaspare Campari conceived the bitterest of the red liqueurs in Novara. He eventually moved to Milan, where the liqueur grew to fame at his Caffé Campari, which opened in 1867. Composed of a mix of proprietary spices and herbs, grain spirit, and sugar, Campari has since become synonymous with Italian cocktails like the Americano and the Negroni. Ranging from 20 to 28 percent ABV (depending on the country), Campari is bracingly bitter, a bit spicy, and infused with a strong taste of bitter orange.

CONTRATTO BITTER • With a base of grape brandy derived from Italian Barbera grapes, Piedmont-based Contratto's red bitter liqueur has its origins in a recipe from 1933. It's similar to Campari in that it's best used in drinks like the Americano and Negroni, but is less aggressively bitter and sweet with a more subtle, herbal backbone owing to a cold maceration of twenty-four different spices and herbs including aloe, hibiscus, wormwood, and juniper. It's coloured naturally with beets and has an ABV of 22 percent.

CAPPELLETTI APERITIVO AMERICANO • Part of Eric Seed's Haus Alpenz portfolio in the United States, Cappelletti is a trebbiano wine–based Americano (see page 14) that combines both sweet and bitter in what is essentially a ready-to-drink cocktail base. It's been made near Trento at the base of the Dolomites since the early twentieth century, where it's known and bottled as Specialino. Cappelletti drinks like a combination of a red bitter and vermouth—all vanilla, sweet grapefruit, and bitter orange— and is a dream ingredient if you like your spritzes with a bit more junk in the trunk. If you can't find Cappelletti, you could use ¾ Campari and ¼ Cocchi or bianco vermouth.

APEROL • Though Aperol defies the red bitter category with its orange hue and sweeter flavour profile, it still contains the subtle bitter element that the spritz requires. First created in 1919 by the Barbieri brothers in Padua, the 11 percent ABV liqueur's secret recipe has, purportedly, remained unchanged for the past century. The main flavour here is sweet grapefruit with aromas of rhubarb and orange.

CONTRATTO APERITIF • Coloured with natural carrot and beet extracts, Contratto aperitif is made from a recipe that dates back to 1935. At 13.5 percent ABV, this orange bitter (similar in style to Aperol) is brandy-based, infused with everything from wormwood to angelica to orange to juniper, and pleasantly bittersweet and herbaceous.

COCCHI AMERICANO • Born in Asti in 1891, Cocchi Americano is an aromatized wine steeped with bitter orange, cinchona bark, and gentian. It's slightly bittersweet with citrus, floral, and herbal notes, and is pale straw yellow in colour. Though it's been on the market continuously since its conception, it's seen a surge in popularity since the 1970s, when the Bava family took over production.

LILLET BLANC AND ROSÉ • Born in Bordeaux in the 1870s, Lillet once referred to Kina Lillet, a quinine-fortified aperitif wine, which eventually fell out of fashion before evolving into, simply, Lillet. Both expressions are made from Sémillion grapes and offer enough sweetness and viscosity to add real texture to a spritz. While the blanc skews more golden and honeyed, the rosé is fresh with notes of berry and citrus.

PUNT E MES • Somewhere between a red bitter, a vermouth, and an amaro, Punt e Mes is the Piedmontese equivalent to a proto-bottled cocktail. It was originally made by the Carpano family (of vermouth fame) starting in the late nineteenth century, and is now owned by Fratelli Branca (which is perhaps most famous for its bracingly bitter Fernet Branca). *Punt e mes* means "one point and a half," which supposedly refers to one part sweet and half part bitter, a phrase which was mirrored and requested by patrons with the gesture of one finger and a thumb.

SUZE • Bitter and herbaceous, Suze is a bright yellow nineteenth-century French aperitif flavoured with wild gentian root. At 15 percent ABV, it slides into the bitter category with a less astringent flavour profile but works in the same manner when paired with white wine, prosecco, stone fruits, and citrus.

GRAN CLASSICO • Golden brown and flavoured with a proprietary mix of herbs and spices including gentian, wormwood, and hyssop, this Swiss-produced aperitif has a bitter bite softened with its herbaceous and caramel-driven backbone. It's most often used as a substitute for Campari.

AMARI • These bitter herbal Italian liqueurs, usually reserved for after a meal thanks to their dark and heavier profile, appear in many of the following recipes thanks to the bite and viscosity lent by sugar and time in the barrel. We recommend stocking Cynar, an artichoke-based formula that's dark but balanced; Braulio, an Alpine amaro with a distinct pine and menthol flavor; and Averna, a sweeter but versatile Sicilian amaro, that works well with brown spirits. We also love Amaro Montenegro (sweeter and mellow) and Amaro Nardini (higher-proof, minty, and intense).

Vermouth, Sherry, and Table Wine

WINE • The most accessible spritz of all—the white wine spritzer—consists of simply a pour of basic white wine mixed with soda water and, if you're feeling fancy, a slice of citrus. Many establishments in Italy still use white wine for their Aperol Spritz instead of prosecco, relying on soda water to add the sparkle. When it comes to still whites, opt for something acidic with just enough stuffing to add texture—like Soave from Italy. When a spritz calls for red wine, a full-bodied red with minimal oak influence—like an un-oaked Cabernet from just about anywhere—does the trick.

SHERRY • Dry styles of sherry, notably fino, manzanilla, and amontillado, are excellent alternatives to the classic white wine base. Fino and manzanilla are both dry and saline, offering a savoury note and bit of perceived acidity, while amontillado offers the same dryness with a kick of oxidation.

VERMOUTH • The original vermouth—a fortified wine aromatized with herbs and spices—was conceived by herbalist Antonio Benedetto Carpano in Turin in 1786. As it became commercially available in the early nineteenth century, Carpano (and many other budding brands like Martini & Rossi) was served in Turin's cafes, helping shape the tradition and ritual of aperitivo. There are a number of vermouth styles beyond those listed below, but these are a solid base to build on when considering your spritz bar.

DRY VERMOUTH • Synonymous with French vermouth, dry vermouth is exactly what it sounds like: dry, spicy, and slightly herbal. Created by Noilly Prat in Marseilles in the early 1800s, the style is now produced by most major vermouth houses. Our favourite dry vermouth brands are Dolin Dry, Noilly Prat, and the newer Carpano Dry.

SWEET VERMOUTH • Sweet Vermouth implies either Vermouth di Torino (which is the original vermouth and is geographically protected) or a vermouth made in the spicy Turin style. Recommended are Carpano

Antica, a centuries-old vanilla-forward recipe from Turin; Cocchi di Torino, a classic formula containing a moscato base; and Dolin Rouge, a Chambéry-style (i.e., drier and lighter) take on sweet vermouth.

VERMOUTH BIANCO/BLANC • Bianco or blanc vermouth is a type of white sweet vermouth that was created in Chambéry, France (the only other town outside of Turin whose vermouths are geographically protected), in 1821. Generally more floral than its red counterparts, bianco or blanc vermouth is best when balanced with herbal flavours and citrus. We love Contratto Bianco, Dolin Blanc, and Carpano Bianco.

Fruit Liqueurs, Syrups, Shrubs, and Infusions

The simplest way to add viscosity and flavour to a basic spritz is to integrate seasonal flavours. Outside of the raw ingredient itself, fruit liqueurs are the most readily available and shelf-stable ingredients to translate fruit flavour to a drink. While most liqueurs on the market are flavour facsimiles (like red-flavoured Skittles) and are usually the colour of neon crayons, Giffard, a French spirits company that dates back to the nineteenth century, makes pure fruit liqueurs that are available across the United States and in the United Kingdom. We use their Pamplemousse Rose (pink grapefruit), Crème de Frais des Bois (wild strawberry), and Framboise (raspberry) the most.

Though bottled liqueurs are available year round (and last nearly forever), their fresh, homemade counterparts are an invaluable addition to the spritz arsenal, capturing the truest essence of a season, fruit, or herb. Both syrups and shrubs (vinegar-based syrups) have the ability to brighten a cocktail with only a dash or two, turning a one-dimensional drink into something far more complex (see page 52).

On the same note, infusing or steeping a spirit base or vermouth with a herb, spice, or fruit provides an extra layer of flavour, translated best through white vermouths, lighter aromatized wines, or clear spirits (see Basil-Infused Dolin Blanc on page 125 or Caraway-Infused Cocchi Americano on page 72). Though the extra step of infusion may seem like a hassle, it takes only a little forethought and a minute or two of preparation. On the next page, find ideas for syrups and shrubs that go well in a spritz.

SYRUPS

CRANBERRY SHRUB

YIELD Approximately 2 cups

1 CUP APPLE CIDER VINEGAR
1 CUP WATER
1 CUP SUGAR
½ CUP FROZEN CRANBERRIES

Add apple cider vinegar, water, sugar, and frozen cranberries in a saucepan over medium-high heat. Bring to a boil, stir, and reduce the heat and simmer for 10 minutes, or until the sugar has dissolved, crushing the cranberries occasionally to release their juices. Cool, strain, bottle, and refrigerate for up to one month.

GINGER SYRUP

YIELD Approximately 1 cup

½ CUP FRESH GINGER JUICE
½ CUP SUGAR

Combine the juice and sugar in a saucepan over very low heat until the sugar is dissolved. Remove from the heat and let sit for at least 30 minutes. Bottle and store in the refrigerator for up to one month.

GRAPE SYRUP

YIELD Approximately 1½ cups

2 CUPS PURPLE, SLIPSKIN GRAPES
1 CUP SUGAR
1 CUP WATER

Combine all of the ingredients in a saucepan over low heat. Crush and muddle the grapes and stir until the sugar is dissolved. Remove from the heat and let sit for at least 30 minutes. Strain, bottle, and store in the refrigerator for up to one month.

HONEY SYRUP

YIELD Approximately 1½ cups

1 CUP HONEY
½ CUP WATER

Combine the honey and water in a saucepan over very low heat. Stir until the honey is dissolved. Remove from the heat and let sit for at least 30 minutes. Bottle and store in the refrigerator for up to one month.

LEMON SYRUP

YIELD Approximately 1¼ cups

1 CUP FRESH
LEMON JUICE

1 CUP SUGAR

Combine the lemon juice and sugar in a saucepan over very low heat. Stir until the sugar is dissolved. Remove from the heat and let sit for at least 30 minutes. Bottle and store in the refrigerator for up to one month.

RASPBERRY SYRUP

YIELD Approximately 2 cups

1 CUP RASPBERRIES

2 CUPS SUGAR

1 CUP WATER

In a saucepan, crush and muddle the raspberries. Add the sugar and water and heat over low heat, stirring until the sugar is dissolved. Be careful not to boil, so the raspberries do not burn. Remove from the heat and let sit for at least 30 minutes. Strain, bottle, and store in the refrigerator for up to one month.

SIMPLE SYRUP

YIELD Approximately 1¼ cups

1 CUP SUGAR

1 CUP WATER

Combine the sugar and water in a saucepan over very low heat. Stir until the sugar is dissolved. Remove from the heat and let sit for at least 30 minutes. Bottle and store in the refrigerator for up to one month.

VANILLA SYRUP

YIELD Approximately 1¼ cups

1 CUP SUGAR

1 CUP WATER

1 VANILLA POD

Combine the sugar and water in a saucepan. Split open the vanilla with a small knife and scrape the contents into the pan; add the bean pod. Turn the heat on low and stir until the sugar is dissolved. Remove from the heat and let sit for at least 30 minutes. Strain, bottle, and store in the refrigerator for up to one month.

CLASSIC

Still drunk daily in their birthplaces like an offering to Italy's aperitivo gods, the classics are the simplest, most traditional of spritz formulas: wine, soda water, and bitter.

VENETIAN SPRITZ

GLASS rocks or wine glass • GARNISH olive and orange half-wheel

2 OUNCES
BITTER LIQUEUR
(SEE NOTE)

3 TO 4 OUNCES
PROSECCO

2 OUNCES
SODA WATER

The spritz that launched a thousand spritzes, the Venetian Spritz is made with a range of bitter liqueurs, including the ubiquitous Aperol from Padua and the more locally beloved Select (thought to be the original bitter used in the Venetian Spritz). Always garnished with a skewered olive and a slice of citrus, this style of spritz is the most widely recognized classic and the standard-bearer of spritz living across Italy.

Build the ingredients in a rocks or wine glass, over ice, and add the garnish.

NOTE

Aperol is the most popular bitter liqueur used in the spritz; it is also the sweetest. If you prefer a more bracingly bitter spritz, try splitting Aperol with Campari (1:1). And if you can find them, Contratto Aperitif, Contratto Bitter, Mauro Vergano Americano, and Cappelletti Aperitivo Americano are four aperitivo bitters we find ourselves returning to over and over again in this classic formula.

NEGRONI SBAGLIATO

GLASS rocks • GARNISH orange half-wheel

The legendary Bar Basso in Milan (which originally opened in 1933 and moved to its current space in 1947) claims provenance of this buoyant little cousin to the Negroni, whose *sbagliato* addendum means "mistaken" or "incorrect" in Italian. Basso's jovial proprietor Maurizio Stocchetto entertains guests with an origin tale citing his father, Mirko—a legendary midcentury barman and the owner of Bar Basso beginning in 1967—as the "accidental" inventor of the drink in the early 1970s, substituting prosecco for gin. Most impressively, the bar serves its sbagliato in a giant handblown goblet complete with an ice block the size of a car battery.

1 OUNCE CAMPARI

1 OUNCE SWEET VERMOUTH

3 OUNCES PROSECCO

Build the ingredients in a rocks glass over ice and add the garnish.

WHITE SPRITZ

GLASS wine glass • GARNISH seasonal citrus, herbs, or fruit

4 OUNCES DRY WHITE WINE

2 OUNCES SODA WATER

½ OUNCE LEMON SYRUP (PAGE 53)

The first vestige of spritz ancestry, the white spritz or spritz liscio was likely—as the Italian mythos goes—born in Habsburg-occupied northern Italy in the nineteenth century, when Austrian soldiers introduced the practice of adding a spritz of water to the region's wines, in an effort to make them more pleasing to their Riesling-weaned palates. This version, with soda water, emerged in the first years of the twentieth century, and is a malleable blueprint created to suit each drinker's palate. Simply add a splash of homemade syrup or fruit liqueur to a base of white wine and soda, and garnish with abandon.

Build the ingredients in a wine glass over ice and add the garnish.

BICICLETTA

GLASS wine glass • GARNISH lemon half-wheel

1 TO 2 OUNCES
CAMPARI

3 OUNCES
WHITE WINE

SODA WATER

Either a white spritz with the addition of Campari or a Venetian Spritz that calls for white wine instead of prosecco, the Bicicletta is named for the mode of transportation in which its drinkers toddle home after several drinks at the local café. Originating in Lombardia in northwest Italy in the 1930s, it's almost exclusively consumed with Campari everywhere except Brescia.

Build the ingredients in a wine glass over ice and add the garnish.

MODERN

Built with the same blueprint as the classics, modern spritzes embrace alternative spirits and liqueurs, more diverse garnishes, fresh juices, and the architecture of other classic drink families.

ROSÉ ALL DAY

GABRIEL ORTA & ELAD ZVI Broken Shaker, Miami, FL
GLASS wine glass • GARNISH lemon half-wheel and
mint sprig

2 OUNCES ROSÉ

1 OUNCE COCCHI
AMERICANO

1 OUNCE
PAPAYA SHRUB
(SEE RECIPE)

½ OUNCE FRESH
LEMON JUICE

1 OUNCE
PROSECCO

The sunshine-soaked cult of rosé has finally reached
fever pitch and is now making regular appearances in
cocktails all over America and the United Kingdom. Here
it shows up—rather appropriately—in a spritz variation
at Miami Beach's Broken Shaker, a backyard cocktail
grove of palm trees and beautiful pool-goers who line
up for seasonal caipirinhas and mojitos every day of
the year. The rosé creates a background for bittersweet
Cocchi Americano and sweet-and-sour papaya shrub, all
bound together with a dose of prosecco.

Add the rosé, Cocchi, papaya shrub, and lemon juice to
a cocktail shaker. Stir well and strain into a wine glass
filled with ice. Top with the prosecco and add the garnish.

PAPAYA SHRUB

Add 5 to 8 chunks papaya, 1 cup rice wine vinegar, and
¼ cup sugar to a saucepan. Simmer over very low heat
for 20 minutes. Cool for at least 30 minutes. Strain,
bottle, and refrigerate for up to one month.

TAROCCO SPRITZ

GLASS rocks • GARNISH blood orange wheel

1 OUNCE GIN

½ OUNCE CAPPELLETTI

¾ OUNCE FRESH BLOOD ORANGE JUICE

½ OUNCE FRESH LEMON JUICE

½ OUNCE VANILLA SYRUP (PAGE 53)

2 OUNCES PROSECCO

Inspired by a cocktail from New York City bartender Natasha David, the crimson-coloured Tarocco Spritz is a nod to the flavour and colour of the Sicilian Tarocco orange, often referred to as the "half-blood orange." A mixed-heritage cocktail, this drink has a bumped-up base of gin to match the vibrant bitter aperitivo liqueur Cappelletti. The drink's acidity comes courtesy of blood orange, lemon juice, and prosecco, bound together by the unlikely addition of vanilla, which complements Cappelletti's notes of spice and oxidation.

Add the gin, Cappelletti, orange juice, lemon juice, and vanilla syrup to a cocktail shaker. Add ice and shake until chilled. Strain over fresh ice, top with the prosecco, and add the garnish.

RÏB TÏCKLER

ALEX DAY Nitecap, New York City, NY
GLASS wine glass • GARNISH grapefruit half-wheel

This drink was born out of the idea to create a more sippable, bubbly White Negroni (a variation on the classic using Suze, gin, and Lillet Blanc or blanc vermouth). To start, bartender Alex Day was set on maintaining the White Negroni's most distinctive element—bitter, gentian-forward Suze. From there, he built in a sour recipe with lemon juice, St-Germain, and simple syrup, and maintained its backbone with dry, spicy Dolin. Though the drink doesn't contain a traditional prosecco topper, it has the lighthearted spritz spirit with its bittersweet twinge, sunshine yellow hue, and bubbly personality.

2 OUNCES DOLIN DRY VERMOUTH

¾ OUNCE SUZE

½ OUNCE ST-GERMAIN

½ OUNCE FRESH LEMON JUICE

¼ OUNCE SIMPLE SYRUP (PAGE 53)

SODA WATER

Pour the vermouth, Suze, St-Germain, lemon juice, and simple syrup in a wine glass over ice. Top with soda water and add the garnish.

VIKING CULTURE

NATASHA DAVID created for Sunshine Co., Brooklyn, NY
GLASS coupe • GARNISH lemon twist

**2 OUNCES
CARAWAY-INFUSED
COCCHI AMERICANO
(SEE RECIPE)**

**¾ OUNCE FRESH
LEMON JUICE**

**¼ OUNCE SIMPLE
SYRUP (PAGE 53)**

**1 TABLESPOON
PEACH CONSERVE
(PREFERABLY
BONNE MAMAN)**

SPARKLING WINE

Charged with conceptualizing a cocktail menu for Sunshine Co., a Brooklyn bar without a full liquor licence, Natasha David was challenged to formulate drinks with the visage of a "real" cocktail, minus the hard spirits. One such result, the Viking Culture, is meant to evoke the flavours of Scandinavia via aquavit and the men "with big, bushy red beards" who drink it, as David puts it. Mimicking aquavit with caraway seed–infused Cocchi Americano, David added the natural flavour pairing of peach, using conserve to create a textural layer. It's all blended together with a good shake and then ushered into sturdy Viking bliss with a topper of sparkling wine.

Add the Cocchi Americano, the lemon juice, simple syrup, and peach conserve to a cocktail shaker. Add ice and shake until chilled. Double-strain into a coupe glass and top with the sparkling wine and garnish.

The remaining infused Cocchi can be added as the base flavour to a simple White Spritz (page 61). Alternatively, the recipe can be halved or quartered and made in a clean, empty bottle to avoid surplus.

CARAWAY-INFUSED COCCHI AMERICANO

Mix 2 tablespoons caraway seeds with 750 ml of Cocchi Americano. Let infuse for 2 hours, strain, and rebottle.

ALPINE SPRITZ

GLASS double rocks or wine glass • GARNISH rosemary sprig

¾ OUNCE BRAULIO

1 OUNCE RIESLING

½ OUNCE GRAPE SYRUP (PAGE 52)

3 OUNCES CRÉMANT D'ALSACE

Made with a list of ingredients meant to channel the cool, glacial ferocity of the Alps, this spritz has a base of Braulio, an Italian alpine bitter that tastes of menthol and bittersweet pine. The acidic Riesling, homemade grape syrup, and aromatic rosemary garnish add a layered complexity that continues to linger after the first sip.

Build the ingredients in a double rocks or wine glass over ice and add the garnish.

NERO CHINATO SPRITZ

DANIEL ZACHARCZUK The Varnish, Los Angeles, CA
GLASS Collins • GARNISH 2 to 3 skewered blackberries

4 BLACKBERRIES

¾ OUNCE FRESH
LEMON JUICE

2½ OUNCES
COCCHI AMERICANO

CHAMPAGNE OR
SPARKLING WINE

SODA WATER

Testing dozens of spritzes for this book revealed a universal truth: Cocchi Americano makes every spritz taste and feel good. Like lying-near-a-body-of-sun-warmed-water good, or lounging-in-a-lawn-chair-at-sunset good. The bittersweet quinine-flavoured aperitivo is also the thing that makes this spritz taste like an effervescent blackberry ice lolly. Equal parts cobbler (thanks to the muddled fruit) and Collins-royale (by way of lemon and Champagne), this purple mess of a cocktail is meant for those previously mentioned moments in the sun.

In a Collins glass, muddle the blackberries. Add ice, the lemon juice, and the Cocchi Americano. Top with equal parts Champagne and soda water and add the garnish.

BLOOD ORANGE

MATTHEW BIANCANIELLO Los Angeles, CA
GLASS Champagne flute or wine glass
GARNISH dehydrated blood orange slice
(see recipe) or a thin slice of blood orange

3 OUNCES
SPARKLING
DRY ROSÉ

¾ OUNCE
CAPPELLETTI

1 OUNCE
REDUCED BLOOD
ORANGE JUICE
(SEE RECIPE)

Matthew Biancaniello's speciality is hyperseasonal drinking. Each week, he forages through L.A.'s farmers' markets and green spaces for the best produce available— filling in the gaps with goods from his own garden—and sets it all up like a veritable juice stand (plus booze). This garnet-coloured cousin of the mimosa makes the most of winter's sexiest commodity, blood orange juice, which is further intensified into a reduction and lifted up with a mix of bubbly rosé and the wine-based bitter Cappelletti.

Build the ingredients in a Champagne flute or wine glass over ice. Cut a small slit in the dehydrated blood orange slice and arrange it on the side of the flute.

REDUCED BLOOD ORANGE JUICE

Pour 1.1 litre Moro blood orange juice into a saucepan and simmer over low heat for 30 to 45 minutes or until it has reduced to 1 cup. Store extra in the fridge for up to one week.

DEHYDRATED BLOOD ORANGE SLICE

Slice a blood orange into 1/8-inch slices and place them in a dehydrator for 8 hours.

UNNAMED
GO-TO

**2-ISH OUNCES
COCCHI AMERICANO**

**½-ISH OUNCE
FINO SHERRY**

**1 TEASPOON OR SO
FRESH LEMON JUICE**

**2 DASHES
BITTERMENS ORANGE
CREME CITRATE**

**2 OUNCES
TONIC WATER**

**2 OUNCES CAVA
OR PROSECCO**

GREG BEST Atlanta, GA • GLASS large tumbler or highball
GARNISH orange, lemon, and lime peels

Greg Best's Unnamed Go-To may be the formula
that comes closest—philosophically speaking—to the
ideal modern spritz recipe. Experimental, somewhat
haphazard, and undeniably refreshing, this cooling
mixture is the definition of insouciant style.

Unceremoniously (and without regard to "making a
mess") assemble all ingredients over crappy refrigerator
ice in a large tumbler. If need be, add more of either or
both bubbly components to fill the glass. Add a large,
hastily cut orange peel as well as that of a lemon or
lime. Haul ass out to the pool where friends are already
drinking cheap cold canned beer. Make all envious.

PUNCH HOUSE SPRITZ

GLASS rocks or wine glass • GARNISH grapefruit half-wheel

2 OUNCES COCCHI AMERICANO

4 OUNCES LINI LAMBRUSCO ROSATO

1 OUNCE FRESH GRAPEFRUIT JUICE

1 OUNCE SODA WATER

Everyone should have a house spritz—a seasonal standard whose proportions are known by heart and ingredients are stocked easily. This is ours. A simple riff on the classic spritz formula originally built to highlight Lini's fruity, irresistible lambrusco rosato, this has become a spring-summer staple for both of us. Gentian-tinged Cocchi Americano plays the bitter role, while sour grapefruit acts as a foil to its sweetness, simultaneously pumping up the volume on the lambrusco. Built in a pitcher or portioned out in a wine glass, it's a drink that embodies the spritz philosophy of being both beautiful and simple.

Build the ingredients in a rocks or wine glass over ice and add the garnish.

LARGE BATCH VARIATION

Combine 3 cups lambrusco rosé, 1½ cups Cocchi Americano, and ¾ cups fresh grapefruit juice in a pitcher. Divide the mixture between 4-6 ice-filled glasses. Top each with 1-2 ounces soda water. Garnish with a grapefruit wheel.

APPENNINI SPRITZ

ADAM BERNBACH 2 Birds 1 Stone, Washington, D.C.
GLASS rocks • **GARNISH** orange half-wheel with seasonal fruit

1 OUNCE COCCHI
BAROLO CHINATO

1 OUNCE
CAPPELLETTI

2 OUNCES CAVA
(IF SUBSTITUTING
PROSECCO,
ADD ½ OUNCE
LEMON JUICE)

Admittedly obsessed with the luscious, bitter allure of Barolo Chinato, Adam Bernbach saw an opportunity to introduce the quinine-fortified wine to the classic Negroni Sbagliato template. Here, he switches the traditional sweet vermouth element for Cocchi's Barolo Chinato and matches it to the wine-based red bitter Cappelletti. The cocktail borrows its name from the chain of mountains that run the length of peninsular Italy, the Apennines.

Build the ingredients in a rocks glass over ice and add the garnish.

HUGO SPRITZ

GLASS wine glass • GARNISH mint sprig and lemon wheel

Reportedly born in South Tyrol along the Italian-Austrian border, the Hugo is a sort of modern incarnation of the white spritz, and a regional competitor to the Aperol Spritz. It was first conceived in the mid-aughts by South Tyrolean Roland Gruber, who originally used lemon syrup, rather than the more common *sciroppo di sambuco* (elderflower syrup), often called *acqua santa* (holy water) locally.

½ OUNCE
ST-GERMAIN

MINT SPRIG

4 OUNCES
PROSECCO

1 OUNCE
SODA WATER

It's since become a regional phenomenon, having been commercially co-opted by an Italian company and bottled as a ready-to-drink cocktail, but the original is still a staple in Austria and Germany. Because fresh elderflower is rarely available, the most widely available replacement is a splash of St-Germain elderflower liqueur.

Add the St-Germain and mint sprig to a wine glass. Gently muddle together and let sit for 3 minutes. Add ice, the prosecco, and the soda water. Stir gently to combine and add the garnish.

AMARENA SPRITZ

2 BRANDIED CHERRIES
(PREFERABLY FABBRI
AMARENA) OR
3 FRESH CHERRIES,
STONED

1 TEASPOON
HIGH-QUALITY
BALSAMIC VINEGAR

1 OUNCE PUNT E MES

1 OUNCE
CARPANO BIANCO

2 OUNCES PROSECCO

2 OUNCES
SODA WATER

GLASS Collins or rocks • GARNISH 2 to 3 brandied cherries (preferably Fabbri Amarena)

The Amarena Spritz combines three northern Italian traditions into one drink: Punt e Mes and Carpano Bianco vermouths from Piedmont, wild brandied amarena cherries from Bologna (though fresh, black cherries are a lovely substitute come summer), and balsamic vinegar from Modena. The brandied cherry syrup and vinegar form a proto-shrub whose sweet-sour nature is a savoury foil to Carpano Bianco and bitter, spicy Punt e Mes.

In a Collins or rocks glass, muddle the cherries with the balsamic vinegar. Add the Punt e Mes, the Carpano Bianco, and ice. Top with the prosecco and soda water and add the garnish.

BYRRH IT'S COLD OUTSIDE

NATASHA DAVID Nitecap, New York City, NY
GLASS Collins • GARNISH lemon wheel

¾ OUNCE BYRRH
GRAND QUINQUINA

¾ OUNCE LUSTAU
AMONTILLADO
SHERRY

½ OUNCE
ANCHO-INFUSED
MOSCATEL SHERRY
(SEE RECIPE)

¾ OUNCE
CRANBERRY
SHRUB (PAGE 52)

½ OUNCE FRESH
LEMON JUICE

1½ OUNCES
SPARKLING WINE

From a winter menu at NYC's Nitecap, the Byrrh It's Cold Outside is a punny moniker for a rather serious spritz. Two intense sherries—one infused with the slow burn of ancho chile—meet Byrrh, the wine and mistelle-based French quinquina wine, and cranberries, whose deep sour quality is preserved in apple cider vinegar. While all of these ingredients might seem oddly matched, the earthy complexity of both sherries combined with the fruity brightness of Byrrh and cranberry is a curiously warming and balanced mix perfect for a cold winter night.

Add the Byrrh, sherries, shrub, and lemon juice to a cocktail shaker with ice. Shake briefly, and strain into a Collins glass over crushed ice. Top with the sparkling wine and add garnish.

ANCHO-INFUSED MOSCATEL SHERRY

Chop a dried ancho chilli in half and remove the seeds. Submerge the seeded chilli in a 750 ml bottle of sherry and let infuse for 2 hours. Strain, rebottle, and refrigerate for up to one month. Infused sherry can also be used for any cocktail recipe that calls for moscatel sherry, or as a spicy sweetener for classic drinks like the Old-Fashioned.

MAi TAi SPRiTZ

MARTIN CATE Smuggler's Cove, San Francisco, CA
GLASS Collins • **GARNISH** mint sprig and lime wheel

½ OUNCE FRESH
LIME JUICE

½ OUNCE ORGEAT

½ OUNCE PIERRE
FERRAND DRY
ORANGE CURAÇAO

1 OUNCE DENIZEN
MERCHANT'S
RESERVE RUM (OR
APPLETON ESTATE
RESERVE RUM)

4 OUNCES CHILLED
BRUT CHAMPAGNE

Like the many maligned Mai Tai recipes floating about
in the cocktail ether, the originator of this tiki classic
has been muddied, with accounts naming Don the
Beachcomber and others fingering his rival, Victor
"Trader Vic" Bergeron. Either way, Vic's version is
the one that lingers as the canonical formula. Austere
compared to many kitchen sink–style tiki drinks, the
Mai Tai pairs lime, almond syrup (orgeat), dry curacao,
and, often, two styles of rum—Jamaican and Martinican.
Martin Cate's spritz-ified version pares down the rum
content in lieu of a Champagne topper in a nod to Trader
Vic's French heritage.

Combine the lime juice, orgeat, curaçao, and rum in a
small container and refrigerate for an hour or two. Pour
the chilled mixture into a Collins glass, fill to the rim with
ice, top with Champagne, and add the garnish.

SPRITZZ

JIM MEEHAN PDT, New York City, NY
GLASS rocks • GARNISH orange half-wheel

2 OUNCES
PELLEGRINO
ARANCIATA

1½ OUNCES
ZWACK AMARO

2 OUNCES
PROSECCO

Jim Meehan created this melding of Italo-Hungarian ingredients for the Caffé della Posta in Bolgheri, Italy, in 2011. Zwack siblings Sandor and Izabella (who produce Zwack amaro and Unicum in Hungary) opened the café in the town where they spent summers until 1987. Upon invitation, Meehan crafted a menu for them that would wed their portfolio with that of Italy's own iconic ingredients. With a flavour reminiscent of caramelized citrus rinds, this cocktail was originally called the Carducci Spritz, so named for the Italian poet Giosuè Carducci who hailed from Tuscany.

Build the ingredients over ice in a rocks glass and add the garnish.

VİVA ALBERTİ

WILL ELLIOTT Maison Premiere, Brooklyn, NY
GLASS wine glass • **GARNISH** orange twist

1 OUNCE STREGA

½ OUNCE COGNAC

1 TEASPOON
CAPPELLETTI

½ OUNCE FRESH
LEMON JUICE

3 DASHES
ANGOSTURA
ORANGE BITTERS

HIGH-QUALITY
SPARKLING WINE

The base ingredient in Will Elliott's complex spritz is the idiosyncratic saffron-infused Strega, a brilliant yellow bitter liqueur whose name means "witch" in Italian. Named after Giuseppe Alberti, who founded the Strega distillery in 1860 in Benevento, Italy, this herbal, savoury spritz boldly carries his name forth.

Add the Strega, cognac, Cappelletti, lemon juice, and bitters to a wine glass. Add cracked ice and stir until chilled. Top with sparkling wine and add the garnish.

WILDAIR SPRITZ

JORGE RIERA Wildair, New York City, NY
GLASS wine glass • **GARNISH** orange twist

This naturalist take on the spritz has become a staple at the New York natural wine bar Wildair. A combination of Mauro Vergano Americano, which is made from Grignolino grapes sourced from Piedmontese natural wine producer Cascina Tarijn, and Les Capriades Pet'Sec—a dry, slightly cloudy pétillant naturel (natural) sparkling wine from the Loire Valley. Wine director Jorge Riera first encountered a version of the drink at the wedding of Loire winemaker Thierry Puzelat, when Puzelat decadently suggested pouring a little of Vergano's aperitivo into a glass of Emmanuel Lassaigne's brut Champagne. (If you cannot find Capriades Pet'Sec, try subbing in a col fondo-style prosecco. See page 40.)

2 OUNCES VERGANO AMERICANO

LES CAPRIADES PET'SEC, TO TOP

To a wine glass, add 3 cubes of ice. Add the Vergano Americano, and top with Pet'Sec. Garnish with an orange twist.

EVERYTHiNG'S COMiNG UP ROSÉ

NATASHA DAVID Nitecap, New York City, NY
GLASS wine glass • **GARNISH** lemon wheel, grapefruit slice, and edible flowers

2 OUNCES
DRY ROSÉ

1 OUNCE
LILLET ROSÉ

1 OUNCE
HIBISCUS TEA

½ OUNCE FRESH
LEMON JUICE

½ OUNCE SIMPLE
SYRUP (PAGE 53)

¼ OUNCE APEROL

1 OUNCE
SPARKLING WINE

This explosion of flower-garnished pinkness was inspired by a traditional sangria template, but instead of white or red wine, Natasha David swapped in rosé and layered it with a splash of bitter Aperol and the subtly sweet punch of Lillet Rosé. Hibiscus tea comes into play with a dry floral note, which is all smoothed together with a little citrus and a topper of sparkling wine.

Pour the rosé, Lillet Rosé, tea, lemon juice, simple syrup, and Aperol over three ice cubes in a wine glass. Top with more ice and sparkling wine and add the garnish.

SAFE PASSAGE

KENENIAH BYSTROM Essex, Seattle, WA
GLASS coupe • GARNISH 2 Castelvetrano olives

1 OUNCE AMARO
NARDINI

¼ OUNCE APEROL

¼ OUNCE FRESH
LEMON JUICE

¼ OUNCE
CASTELVETRANO
OLIVE BRINE

2½ OUNCES
PROSECCO

This drink is a riff on another cocktail called the Sweet
Olive, which hails from the beloved Brooklyn restaurant
Franny's. Keneniah Bystrom created the Safe Passage
to guide his restaurant through a party in honour of
Franny's recently released cookbook. Swapping the
Sweet Olive's Meletti Amaro for Amaro Nardini—which
is infused with bitter gentian and fresh peppermint—
Bystrom created a softly bitter spritz whose salty
complexity matches the sweet citrus of Aperol and the
bitter twinge of Nardini.

Add Amaro Nardini, Aperol, lemon juice, and olive
brine to a cocktail shaker. Add ice and shake until
chilled. Strain into a chilled coupe or cocktail glass.
Top with prosecco and garnish with olives.

APEROL BETTY

TERRONI, Los Angeles, CA • **GLASS** Collins or rocks
GARNISH orange wheel

2 OUNCES APEROL

1 OUNCE FRESH
ORANGE JUICE

½ OUNCE FRESH
GRAPEFRUIT JUICE

3 OUNCES PROSECCO

The Aperol Betty is barely more than a glorified,
bittersweet Mimosa. At Terroni in Los Angeles, Aperol
is mixed with fresh orange and grapefruit juices, both
of which freshen up the liqueur's bite, and then topped
with prosecco for a cooler-style spritz that is appropriate
morning, noon, or night.

Add all ingredients to a cocktail shaker, add ice and
shake. Strain over ice into a rocks or Collins glass.
Top with prosecco and garnish with an orange wheel.

COUSINS

A more avant-garde breed, the spritz cousins adapt a wider variety of ingredients and techniques than the classic or modern, but embody the same bubbly, bitter, easy-going spirit.

AMERICANO

GLASS Collins • GARNISH orange half-wheel

Though popular history dictates that the Americano was named for the American tourists who took to the eye-catching crimson aperitivo, it's more likely that the name derives from the word *amer*, which means "bitter" in Italian. But before it was ever called the Americano, and before it included soda water, it was the Milano-Torino for its base flavours—bitter red Campari and herbaceous sweet vermouth—which hail from Milan and Turin respectively. Invented in the first decades of the twentieth century, the drink is documented for the first time in Ferruccio Mazzon's *Guida al Barman* (1920). It's become one of Italy's most famous mixed drinks, ultimately laying the foundation for the bittersweet Negroni, which was supposedly conceived in the 1930s in Florence.

1½ OUNCES
CAMPARI

1½ OUNCES
SWEET VERMOUTH

SODA WATER

Pour the Campari and vermouth into a Collins glass over ice. Top with soda water and add the garnish.

AMERICANO PERFECTO

DAMON BOELTE Grand Army Bar, Brooklyn, NY
GLASS Collins • GARNISH orange wheel

1½ OUNCES
CAMPARI

¾ OUNCE
DOLIN ROUGE

¾ OUNCE
CARPANO ANTICA

4 OUNCES PILSNER

Damon Boelte's clever twist on the Americano turns the traditional aperitivo into a Franco-Italian shandy. Where the standard Americano pairs equal parts bitter Campari with sweet vermouth, the Perfecto splits the sweet in half with two different vermouths—brutish Carpano and the fruitier French Dolin Rouge—to create a more nuanced sweetness. The traditional topper of soda water is then replaced with pilsner beer for a refreshing, malty, bittersweet beer cocktail.

Pour the Campari and vermouths into a Collins glass over ice. Slowly top with the pilsner and add the garnish.

COFFEE SPRITZ

GLASS Collins

2 OUNCES
SODA WATER

¾ OUNCE AVERNA

½ OUNCE AGED
RUM (PREFERABLY
FLOR DE CAÑA 12)

½ OUNCE VANILLA
SYRUP (PAGE 53)

1½ OUNCES COLD-
BREWED COFFEE

1 EGG WHITE

PROSECCO

Coffee is perhaps not the most intuitive base for a spritz, but this drink takes its inspiration from the traditional Italian pre-aperitivo—afternoon espresso—and manages to make it surprisingly brunch-appropriate. Dark, rich Sicilian amaro combines with aged rum and vanilla syrup to form a base not unlike root beer. With the addition of cold-brewed coffee and egg white, it becomes nearly a coffee float, which is fully realized with a topper of soda water and sparkling wine. Altogether, this creamy cocktail has the feeling of an old-fashioned chocolate egg cream, with an Italian soul.

Pour the soda water into a Collins glass.

Combine the Averna, rum, syrup, coffee, and egg white in a cocktail shaker and shake without ice. Add ice and shake until chilled. Strain into a Collins glass and let sit for 10 seconds, then top with prosecco until foam rises above the glass.

PUNCH ROMAINE

GLASS snifter or rocks • GARNISH orange peel

1 EGG WHITE

1 OUNCE WHITE RUM

½ OUNCE SIMPLE SYRUP (PAGE 53)

½ OUNCE FRESH LEMON JUICE

1 OUNCE FRESH ORANGE JUICE

CHAMPAGNE OR SPARKLING WINE

Served as the sixth course of the *Titanic*'s final first-class dinner, the Punch Romaine's claim to fame is a rather morbid one. Had it not been the palate cleanser between the meat and squab courses that April evening, it might have been better remembered for its famous originator—French chef Georges Auguste Escoffier—or the fact that it's an utterly divine, citrusy aperitif. The original Punch Romaine took more the form of a granita—a popular in-between course in those years—than a cocktail, but here it's been updated to a frothy spritz served over a heaping mound of crushed ice.

Combine the egg white, rum, simple syrup, lemon juice, and orange juice in a cocktail shaker. Shake without ice, and then add ice and shake again until chilled. Strain over crushed ice into a snifter, top with Champagne, and add the garnish.

SENSA SPRITZ

GLASS Collins • GARNISH cucumber ribbon or spear

PINCH SEA SALT

½ OUNCE SIMPLE SYRUP (PAGE 53)

2 CUCUMBER SLICES

¾ OUNCE SALERS

¾ OUNCE DOLIN DRY VERMOUTH

½ OUNCE FRESH LIME JUICE

SODA WATER

Each spring, for over a thousand years, Venice has celebrated its Festa della Sensa, or the city's marriage to the sea. A ritual that recognizes the island people's dependence on the Adriatic for their livelihood, Sensa was, and still is, initiated with a parade of boats and the tossing of a gold ring into the sea on the day of the Ascension. Meant to evoke the lagoon waters surrounding Venice, the Sensa Spritz is cool, dry, and mildly bitter with a base of Salers, a French aperitif, and dry vermouth bound together with the cooling herbaceousness of cucumber.

In a cocktail shaker, muddle the sea salt and simple syrup with the cucumber slices. Add the Salers, vermouth, and lime juice. Add ice and shake until chilled. Strain into a Collins glass over ice, top with soda water, and add the garnish.

SHORE LEAVE SPRITZ

1½ OUNCES COCCHI AMERICANO

½ OUNCE PERRY'S TOT GIN

¾ OUNCE FRESH LIME JUICE

¾ OUNCE FRESH GRAPEFRUIT JUICE

½ OUNCE HONEY SYRUP (PAGE 52)

½ TEASPOON VANILLA SYRUP (PAGE 53)

½ TEASPOON ALLSPICE DRAM

1 OUNCE SODA WATER

MATTHEW BELANGER Donna, Brooklyn, NY
GLASS hurricane • GARNISH grapefruit half-wheel and a cinnamon stick

Matt Belanger likes to "shoehorn tiki into everything," as he puts it, which is reflected in the perpetually tropical cocktail menu at Brooklyn's Donna. Based on tiki baron Don the Beachcomber's 1941 recipe for Navy Grog, this drink stays true to its maritime origins but lightens the usual three-ounce rum base in favour of a small dose of navy-strength gin and Cocchi Americano to create the sort of spicy, juicy cocktail you'd want to drink while on dry land.

Combine the Cocchi Americano, gin, lime juice, grapefruit juice, honey syrup, vanilla syrup, and allspice dram into a cocktail shaker. Add ice and shake briefly. Strain over crushed ice into a hurricane glass, top with the soda water, and add the garnish.

ROME WITH A VIEW

MICHAEL MCILROY Attaboy, New York City, NY
GLASS Collins • **GARNISH** orange half-wheel

1 OUNCE CAMPARI

1 OUNCE DRY VERMOUTH

1 OUNCE FRESH LIME JUICE

¾ OUNCE SIMPLE SYRUP (PAGE 53)

SODA WATER

A riff on the Americano blueprint, the Rome with a View substitutes dry vermouth for sweet and builds a sour formula into the tall cooler, giving it a kicky vibe. Bracingly bittersweet, it nearly conjures warm late afternoons looking out over the Eternal City. Michael McIlroy's lit-minded cocktail is so slurpable and eye-catching, it's become something of a modern classic on the East Coast.

Combine the Campari, vermouth, lime juice, and simple syrup in a cocktail shaker. Add ice and shake until chilled. Strain over ice into a Collins glass, top with soda water, and add the garnish.

SiPPY CUP

LEO ROBITSCHEK The NoMad, New York City, NY
GLASS highball • GARNISH orange half-wheel
and 3 mint sprigs

¾ OUNCE GINGER
SYRUP (PAGE 52)

1 OUNCE FRESH
LIME JUICE

1 OUNCE COCCHI
VERMOUTH DI
TORINO

1½ OUNCES
AVERNA

2 DASHES
ANGOSTURA
BITTERS

1 OUNCE
SODA WATER

While giving this recipe a test run, Leo Robitschek tried it
out on a friend who declared the kicky gingery result so
drinkable that even a kid would like it. He then suggested it
might be served in a sippy cup to his own two rambunctious
children—who were also present—to calm them down.
Of course they did no such thing, but the name stuck. A
combination of sweet vermouth, Sicilian amaro, tart lime,
and extra-peppery ginger syrup, the Sippy Cup is fit for
all thirsty adults in need of a little sedating.

Combine the ginger syrup, lime juice, vermouth, and
Averna in a cocktail shaker. Add ice and shake. Strain into
a highball glass over ice. Add Angostura and top with the
soda water. Pinch the orange half-wheel together and
skewer through the ends. Place the mint sprigs through
the centre and garnish.

WHITE PORT & TONIC

GLASS highball • GARNISH lemon half-wheel
and mint sprig

The Portuguese White Port & Tonic contains the same
aperitivo-driven spirit as the Italian white spritz and the
Spanish gin and tonic. A mash-up of the two, this drink
is a simple mixture of slightly off-dry port made from
white grapes—most often used in pre-dinner cocktails or
punch in Portugal's Douro Valley—and the bracing fresh
and bitter bite of tonic. The result is a simple vinous drink
with a bit more background and punch than the classic
white spritz.

**2 OUNCES
WHITE PORT**

**4 OUNCES TONIC
(PREFERABLY
FEVER TREE)**

**½ OUNCE FRESH
LEMON JUICE**

For a variation with just a bit more intrigue, muddle a
few leaves of mint at the bottom of the glass with a few
dashes of orange bitters and then top with port and tonic.

Build the ingredients in a highball glass over ice and add
the garnish.

TINTO DE VERANO

GLASS snifter • **GARNISH** lemon, orange, or other seasonal fruit

3 OUNCES RED WINE (FULL-BODIED AND DRY)

1 OUNCE LEMON SYRUP (PAGE 53)

SODA, TO TOP

Perhaps the Tinto de Verano (literally "summer red wine") is Spain's equivalent of a basic spritz. There it's cut with *gaseosa*, a lemon-flavoured soda, and can be found already mixed and bottled at the grocery store. Simpler than Sangria and lower in alcohol than the country's other national obsession, the "Gin-Tonic" as they call it, this version freshens up the typical formula with red wine, homemade lemon syrup, and a long pour of soda water for a surprisingly light and poppy Spanish spritz.

Add wine and lemon syrup to a shaker. Add ice and shake gently until chilled. Pour over ice into a tumbler or wine glass. Top with soda and garnish.

SGROPPINO

GLASS small rocks • GARNISH mint sprig

¾ OUNCE VODKA
(PREFERABLY
A CITRUS VODKA
LIKE ST. GEORGE)

½ CUP LEMON
SORBET

1 OUNCE
PROSECCO

In the Venetian dialect, *sgropin*, meaning "to untie," is a play on the duty of the digestivo drink to provide postprandial relief. Supposedly concocted in sixteenth-century Venice as a palate cleanser between courses—in which case it resembled a sorbet more than a cocktail—the Sgroppino has taken on the modern duality of slushy aperitivo cocktail and dessert-y digestivo. It's sometimes made with grappa, but this version uses vodka to let the Veneto's sparkling wine come to the forefront.

Combine all ingredients in a cocktail shaker and whip quickly with a whisk until smooth and uniform in texture. Pour into a small rocks glass and add the garnish.

MONT BLANC FIZZ

DAN SABO Ace Hotel, Los Angeles, CA
GLASS highball • GARNISH orange peel

1 EGG WHITE

1¼ OUNCES
AMARO MELETTI

½ OUNCE
GRAND MARNIER

½ OUNCE FRESH
LEMON JUICE

¼ OUNCE ORGEAT

2 DASHES
ANGOSTURA
BITTERS

SODA WATER

This cocktail was born from Dan Sabo's simple desire to create a sour using the saffron-infused Amaro Meletti. Needing to balance the drink's rich bitterness, Sabo added the cognac-based orange liqueur Grand Marnier, thus uniting two Alpine spirits in one glass. The intensely fluffy head—courtesy of an egg white and a good dry shake (shaking without ice)—bears a resemblance to Europe's highest peak, Mont Blanc.

Combine the egg white, Amaro Meletti, Grand Marnier, lemon juice, orgeat, and bitters in a cocktail shaker and shake without ice. Add a mix of crushed and cubed ice, and shake again until the tin is very cold. Strain into a highball glass. Wait 10 seconds and top with soda water. Add the garnish.

COLD IN THE SHADOWS

PAMELA WIZNITZER Seamstress, New York City, NY
GLASS highball • GARNISH lime wheel and orange wheel

1 OUNCE CAMPARI

½ OUNCE ST. GEORGE
RASPBERRY LIQUEUR

½ OUNCE HONEY
SYRUP (PAGE 52)

1 OUNCE FRESH
LIME JUICE

1½ OUNCES
ANDERSON
VALLEY IPA

An ode to Northern California, the Cold in the Shadows
hints at San Francisco's chilly umbra, even in the warmest
of months. Each ingredient is connected to the region—
the IPA from the Anderson Valley, Campari, whose
headquarters are housed in San Francisco, and St. George
from Alameda—and blended together in what drinks like
a bitter shandy.

Combine the Campari, raspberry liqueur, honey syrup,
and lime juice in a cocktail shaker. Shake quickly with
a couple of ice cubes, then add the IPA. Strain into a
highball glass over crushed ice and add the garnish.

DIAMOND SPRITZ FIZZ

1½ OUNCES
APEROL

¼ OUNCE FRESH
LEMON JUICE

½ OUNCE DOLIN
DRY VERMOUTH

½ OUNCE HONEY
SYRUP (PAGE 52)

¼ OUNCE GRAN
CLASSICO BITTER
AMARO

1 TEASPOON FRESH
ORANGE JUICE

1 EGG WHITE

2½ OUNCES
SPARKLING WINE

ISAAC SHUMWAY created for Tosca, San Francisco, CA
GLASS Collins • GARNISH orange twist

The Diamond Fizz was born around the turn of this century, when the fizz was hitting the big time in American bars. A deceptively strong and highly drinkable mixture, it replaces the Gin Fizz's soda water with Champagne, transforming it into a royale of sorts. Isaac Shumway's spritz-ified version replaces the gin with Aperol and dry vermouth, the sugar with honey syrup and amaro, and the lemon juice with orange juice. The result is a fluffy orange cloud of a cocktail that tastes something like a bitter Orange Julius.

Add the Aperol, lemon juice, vermouth, syrup, Gran Classico, orange juice, and egg white to a cocktail shaker. Shake without ice, and then add ice and shake very hard for 20 seconds. Strain into a Collins glass over a very small amount of ice. Slowly top with the sparkling wine and add the garnish.

SANGRITA

ADAPTED FROM the *Stork Club Bar Book* by Lucius Beebe
GLASS highball • GARNISH pineapple wedge and lime wheel

2 OUNCES RED
WINE

1 OUNCE FRESH
PINEAPPLE JUICE

¾ OUNCE SIMPLE
SYRUP (PAGE 53)

¾ OUNCE FRESH
LIME JUICE

SODA WATER

This drink was a favourite of Jinx Falkenburg, one of America's first supermodels in the 1930s and 1940s, and was—according to her—popular amongst Mexican bullfighters. A regular at New York's star-studded Stork Club, Falkenburg lent this recipe to Lucius Beebe as he was penning the Stork's narrative history, which includes the favourite drinks of a dozen other Broadway and Hollywood icons. Incidentally, the Sangrita is closely related to the Claret Lemonade, another red wine–based cocktail popular in the nineteenth century.

Add the red wine, pineapple juice, simple syrup, and lime juice to a highball glass over ice. Top with soda water and add the garnish.

HUNGRY HUNGRY HIPSTER

TOBY MALONEY The Violet Hour, Chicago, IL
GLASS Collins • GARNISH orange half-wheel

2 OUNCES ZWACK

1 OUNCE FRESH
ORANGE JUICE

¾ OUNCE FRESH
LEMON JUICE

MILLER HIGH LIFE

Several years ago at a sports bar in Williamsburg, Brooklyn—spiritual home of the hipster—bartender Toby Maloney was introduced to the "bro-mosa," an ironic play on the Mimosa consisting of Miller High Life and orange juice. He was happily surprised at how well orange complemented the Champagne of Beers' maltiness, and decided to integrate the discovery into his own bars, where oranges usually languished after being stripped of their peels for garnish. Maloney added another layer of complexity with Zwack, a Hungarian amaro, for a more bitter play on the bro-mosa.

Combine the Zwack, orange juice, and lemon juice in a cocktail shaker. Add ice and shake until chilled. Strain into a Collins glass over ice, top with Miller High Life, and add the garnish.

PINK LEMONADE
À LA PLAYBOY

GLASS Collins or large tumbler • GARNISH lemon wheel
and brandied cherry

2 OUNCES ROSÉ

1 OUNCE FRESH
LEMON JUICE

1 OUNCE FRESH
ORANGE JUICE

½ OUNCE GIFFARD
PAMPLEMOUSSE
ROSE LIQUEUR

SODA WATER

In the 1971 edition of *Playboy's Host & Bar Book* by
Thomas Mario, a recipe for a boozy pink lemonade peers
out between a Pineapple Mint Cooler and a Pink Rum
and Tonic (don't ask). A rosé-based approximation of
Playboy's kitschy blueprint, this drink adds Giffard's pink
grapefruit liqueur for extra depth and texture. Soda
water gives it that all-important sparkle.

Pour the rosé, lemon juice, orange juice, and liqueur into
a Collins glass or large tumbler over ice. Top with soda
water and add the garnish.

TUNNEL VISION

ALEX DAY Death & Co., New York City, NY
GLASS Collins or wine glass • GARNISH basil and lime wheel

2 OUNCES BASIL-
INFUSED DOLIN
BLANC VERMOUTH
(SEE RECIPE)

½ OUNCE PEAR
EAU DE VIE

½ OUNCE FRESH
LIME JUICE

½ OUNCE SIMPLE
SYRUP (PAGE 53)

2 DASHES
ABSINTHE

SODA WATER

The Tunnel Vision was born of Alex Day's desire to create a drink that was simultaneously refreshing and savoury, the latter of which is achieved with herb-infused vermouth and high-proof pear eau de vie. The drink's real inspiration is hidden in its name, a phrase that describes Day's blinding obsession with the combination when he dreamed up this tall, strange beauty.

Combine the vermouth, eau de vie, lime juice, simple syrup, and absinthe in a cocktail shaker. Add ice and shake until chilled. Strain into a Collins glass over ice and add the garnish.

BASIL-INFUSED DOLIN BLANC VERMOUTH
Add 4 to 6 basil leaves to a half bottle, or 8 to 10 leaves to a full 750 ml bottle of Dolin Blanc vermouth. Let infuse for 2 hours, strain, and rebottle. If you don't have time for infusing, gently muddle 4 to 6 basil leaves into the simple syrup.

SECOND SERVE

DAN GREENBAUM Attaboy, New York City, NY
GLASS Collins • GARNISH orange half-wheel

1 OUNCE AMARO
MONTENEGRO

1 OUNCE FINO
SHERRY

1 OUNCE FRESH
LIME JUICE

¾ OUNCE SIMPLE
SYRUP (PAGE 53)

SODA WATER

Built with the sensibility of a Collins (spirit + citrus +
sugar + soda), the Second Serve is Dan Greenbaum's
nod to the soft-hitting elegance of tennis. Crisp,
refreshing fino sherry mixes with sweet, herbal
Montenegro, and is stretched into a cooling, bubbly
aperitivo with piquant lime, sugar, and soda.

Combine the Amaro Montenegro, sherry, lime juice, and
simple syrup in a cocktail shaker. Shake and strain into
a Collins glass over cubed ice. Top with soda water and
add the garnish.

BITTER INTENTIONS

BOBBY HEUGEL Anvil and The Pastry War, Houston, TX
GLASS Collins • GARNISH orange slice

1½ OUNCES
SODA WATER

2 OUNCES
CAMPARI

¾ OUNCE FRESH
LEMON JUICE

¾ OUNCE SIMPLE
SYRUP (PAGE 53)

1 OUNCE
VERMOUTH
(PREFERABLY
CARPANO ANTICA)

Combining the spirit of the Americano with the attitude of a sour, Bobby Heugel's Bitter Intentions is a playful riff on two classic cocktail archetypes. Because Campari can skew sweet, the addition of lemon mellows the combination but still allows the underlying bitter to come through. As always, soda completes and balances the drink, tying it all up with an elegant, bubbly bow.

Pour the soda water into a Collins glass without ice.

Combine the Campari, lemon juice, and simple syrup in a cocktail shaker. Add ice and shake. Strain into the Collins glass over ice. Add cracked ice, top with the vermouth, and add the garnish.

THE APERITIVO TABLE

TECHNICALLY, THE PREDOMINANT RELIGION of Italy is Roman Catholicism, but in reality it's communing over food and drink. Carrots, celery, and onions are the holy trinity; garlic, tomatoes, and basil the patron saints; prosciutto, mortadella, and pecorino the archangels. And wine is—quite obviously—the Messiah.

Say what you may about spirituality, there is nothing more spiritually binding than breaking bread, twirling pasta around a fork, and sharing wine with other humans on a sunny patch of street. (What did you think the Eucharist was about?) Tourists travel to Italy year after year solely to take part in this tradition, as if it wasn't replicable in their own countries. It's just somehow, the world collectively agrees, that Italy does it best, particularly when it comes to that crescent of space between work and play called aperitivo.

Italians abide with unwavering faithfulness by the belief that a little something to eat and drink will foster the appetite and the desire for a little something more. It's a simple creed that, as Roberto Bava of Cocchi very neatly sums up, "is not an invention; it's a need." And when pressed to answer the question of when he guesses this tradition of taking a little pre-dinner bite and a drink originated in Italy, he says, half joking, "Maybe when the first cheese is invented?"

And like Italy's library of cheese, the aperitivo snacks of each region— beyond the perfunctory olives and potato chips—vary depending on the local agriculture, cosmopolitan influence (or lack thereof), and drinking traditions.

In Venice, the snacks that typically accompany a proper aperitivo are called cicchetti. This word—used exclusively in Venice—is derived from the word *ciccus*, meaning "small quantity" in Latin. Served throughout the day and into aperitivo hour, cicchetti most commonly includes things like crostini, fried seafood served on skewers or in paper cones, *polpette* (meatballs), and *sarde in saor* (sardines). But in a new era of satisfying crowds who flock for spritz and its accompanying lifestyle, anything that can be miniaturized, picked up, and eaten is considered cicchetti material.

Across the country in industrious Milan, the two-for-one American style of happy hour began to take hold during the economic downturn of the recent decade, and now food is often included in the price of a drink. Part of the relatively new phenomenon of apericena, the buffet style of service shepherds in passersby with tables covered in everything from pizzette to *mondeghili* (deep-fried Milanese meatballs) to quiches to French fries. (However, if you see French fries on any Italian buffet, it's safe to say you should be spritzing elsewhere.) Thanks to the city's welcoming of international influence, aperitivo food is less Milanese and more pan-continental.

By contrast, Turin is something of a composite of Milan's often Rococo flair and Venice's traditionalism, funnelled through a deeply rooted café culture that remains true to its Piedmontese culinary heritage. Here, you'll find both wine bars and ornate cafés serving little snacks for a euro or two each alongside proprietary vermouth, spritzes, and wine. But you'll also find elaborate buffets loaded with everything from fresh vegetables and *bagna cauda* (anchovy and garlic sauce) to skewered cubes of silky mortadella to composed salads to *vitello tonnato*, a regional speciality of cold, thinly sliced veal smothered in creamy tuna sauce.

And between each of these proud, distinct cities, the nuance continues. But the point is, without food there would be no aperitivo hour in the modern sense. There would be no name for the crescent of space that has been carved out between the end of the workday and the dinner hour. There would be no crescent of space. And there would be no spritz.

SARDE IN SAOR

ADAPTED FROM Polpo, London, UK
SERVES 6–8

One of Venice's most traditional dishes, *sarde in saor* was—since at least the fourteenth century—a way to preserve fish for seamen making long voyages. Today it can still be found across the Floating City's menus at every turn.

20 SMALL SARDINES, CLEANED AND GUTTED

2 CUPS PLAIN FLOUR

1/4 CUP EXTRA-VIRGIN OLIVE OIL, PLUS 2 TABLESPOONS

1/3 CUP PINE NUTS

4 LARGE ONIONS, FINELY SLICED

SEA SALT

3/4 CUP WHITE WINE VINEGAR

1/3 CUP RAISINS, SOAKED IN WATER OVERNIGHT AND DRAINED

TOASTED BAGUETTE OR RUSTIC ITALIAN BREAD

Place a wire rack in a baking sheet lined with paper towels.

Toss the sardines in the flour and shake off any excess. In a large saucepan, heat the 1/4 cup of oil over medium-high heat. Place the floured sardines into the oil and cook (frying in batches if needed) until golden on both sides. Place the fried sardines on the prepared wire rack.

In a small saucepan over low heat, toast the pine nuts, shaking occasionally, until lightly browned, about 1 minute. Set aside to cool.

Add the 2 tablespoons of oil to a large saucepan over medium-low heat and add the sliced onions. Sprinkle with salt and sweat for 20 to 30 minutes, or until soft, sweet, and translucent. Remove from the heat and pour enough white wine vinegar over the onions to fully submerge with extra liquid. Add the raisins and pine nuts.

In a large container with an airtight lid, spread some of the onion mix on the bottom. Add a layer of sardines and sprinkle with a little salt. Add alternate layers of onion and sardines.

Seal the container and store in the refrigerator for 2 days to marinate (will keep for up to 5 days). When ready to serve, bring the sardine mixture up to room temperature and serve with freshly toasted bread.

TRAMEZZINI

The omnipresent Italian snack food, tramezzini are small crustless sandwiches made with white milk–based bread and stuffed with anything from tuna and hard-boiled eggs to porchetta and radicchio, depending on the season and the region. Born in Turin in the 1920s—allegedly at the gilded Caffè Mulassano—tramezzini were the Italian answer to English tea sandwiches, made immediately more appealing by replacing vegetables with things like prosciutto and tea with alcoholic beverages.

Interestingly enough, the tiny sandwiches weren't actually dubbed "tramezzini" until the 1930s, when writer and philosopher Gabriele D'Annunzio supposedly coined the word, which is meant to sound like a combination of *triangolo* (triangle), *tra* (between), and *mezzo* (middle). Milk-based bread was not traditionally prevalent in the Italian diet but became a café staple post World War II, thanks to American and English influences.

CAFFÈ FLORIAN'S TRAMEZZINI

INSPIRED BY those served at Venice's iconic café on St. Mark's Square. • MAKES 8

6 SLICES WHITE SANDWICH BREAD, CRUSTS REMOVED

¼ CUP MAYONNAISE

3 LARGE HARD-BOILED EGGS, THINLY SLICED

6 SLICES PARMA COTTO

Spread three slices of white bread with mayonnaise. Top 1 slice with a layer of egg slices. Place the second piece of bread, mayonnaise side up, on top, creating a new layer. Add a layer of parma cotto, and then place the last slice of bread, mayonnaise side down, on top of that. Slice into 4 triangles and thread, 2 each, on to a large skewer. Repeat with the remaining three bread slices, mayonnaise, egg, and parma cotto.

ITALIAN TUNA SALAD

MAKES 8

2 CANS UNSALTED
ALBACORE TUNA
LOIN IN OIL, DRAINED

4 CASTELVETRANO
OLIVES, STONED
AND FINELY
CHOPPED

3 TABLESPOONS
RED ONION, FINELY
CHOPPED

1 TEASPOON
LEMON ZEST

1 TABLESPOON
FRESH LEMON JUICE

EXTRA-VIRGIN
OLIVE OIL

SALT AND PEPPER,
TO TASTE

ROCKET

4 SLICES WHITE
SANDWICH BREAD,
CRUSTS REMOVED

In a large bowl, break up the tuna with a fork. Add the olives, red onion, lemon zest, lemon juice, and enough oil to coat (about ¼ cup). Season with salt and pepper, and toss to combine.

Arrange a few leaves of rocket on a slice of bread. Top with a few spoonfuls of tuna salad, and spread into an even layer. Add another layer of arugula and top with a second slice of bread. Slice into 4 triangles and thread, 2 each, on to a large skewer. Repeat with the remaining two bread slices, rocket, and tuna.

APERITIVO ESSENZIALE

No matter what sort of establishment you wander into during aperitivo, salty snacks are always on offer, whether a basket of generic potato chips or an elaborate buffet that—excepting aperitivo etiquette—could easily double as dinner. The most satisfying spreads provide a few grazing options with high-quality ingredients and enough cushion to ward off a heavy buzz. This essential setup was inspired by aperitivo hour at the Hotel Bulgari in Milan, a modern resort hidden in an eighteenth-century palazzo surrounded by manicured gardens, where cocktails come with a pretty price tag but the snacks are bottomless and beautifully presented.

OVEN-ROASTED OLIVES

YIELD 2 cups

2 CUPS MIXED OLIVES (PREFERABLY CASTELVETRANO, KALAMATA, AND GAETA)

¼ CUP EXTRA-VIRGIN OLIVE OIL

ORANGE ZEST, GRATED

Heat the oven to 230°C.

In a bowl, combine the olives and 3 tablespoons of the oil, then spread the olives evenly on a parchment paper-lined baking sheet. Roast until just sizzling, about 5 minutes. Remove from the oven and transfer to a small bowl to cool slightly. Add the remaining tablespoon olive oil. Sprinkle the orange zest over the top, toss to combine, and serve warm.

SAFFRON ALMONDS

YIELD 1 cup

1 TABLESPOON
EXTRA-VIRGIN
OLIVE OIL

2 SAFFRON THREADS

1 CUP MARCONA
ALMONDS

Place oil and saffron threads in a saucepan over very low heat. Let sit, stirring occasionally, so the saffron releases its colour and aroma into the oil.

In a separate saucepan, toast the nuts over medium heat until just golden brown, about 2 minutes. Transfer to a bowl and let cool. Add the saffron oil, toss to coat, and serve warm.

HAND-CUT POTATO CHIPS

YIELD Approximately 6 cups

4 RUSSET POTATOES,
WASHED, SCRUBBED,
AND DRIED

4 CUPS VEGETABLE
OIL, FOR FRYING

SEA SALT

Fill a large bowl with cold water. Using a mandoline, thinly slice the potatoes and drop them into the bowl to keep them from browning.

Strain the potato slices and layer them between paper towel sheets, pressing to soak up the water. Keep between paper towels until ready to fry.

Prepare a plate with dry paper towel sheets for the potato chips to rest on after frying.

Place oil in a heavy-bottomed frying pan, and heat to 180°C on a deep-fry thermometer. Using a metal slotted spoon and working in small batches, carefully place the potato slices into the oil, frying until golden, 1 to 2 minutes for each batch. Scoop the finished chips out of the oil with a slotted spoon and place onto the paper towel-lined plate.

Sprinkle with sea salt and serve in a paper bag alongside olives and nuts.

GRISSINI WITH PROSCIUTTO AND PICKLED RADICCHIO

ADAPTED FROM Polpo, London, UK • MAKES 20

¾ CUP
WHITE WINE

¾ CUP WHITE
WINE VINEGAR

4 JUNIPER BERRIES

20 RADICCHIO
LEAVES

½ CUP EXTRA-
VIRGIN OLIVE OIL

20 ITALIAN
GRISSINI
(SEE NOTE)

20 THIN SLICES
OF PROSCIUTTO

In a saucepan, bring the white wine, white wine vinegar, and juniper berries to a boil over medium heat. When the liquid is bubbling, submerge the radicchio leaves and let boil for 5 minutes.

Meanwhile, pour the oil into an airtight container.

Remove the white wine mixture from the heat, remove the radicchio with tongs, and gently shake off any excess liquid. If making ahead of time, place the pickled leaves in the oil and store in the refrigerator until ready to use so that they retain their colour and flavour. Drain the leaves of any excess oil before using.

Starting at the top of each grissini, wrap with a piece of prosciutto, and then wrap with a radicchio leaf. Repeat for all remaining breadsticks.

NOTE

Italian grissini, or breadsticks, can be purchased at Italian grocers and most supermarkets.

CARCIOFI ALLA VENEZIANA

SERVES 4

The sandy lagoon islands surrounding Venice have the muddy soil ideal for growing the artichoke, especially the purple Sant'Erasmo variety. Sold at the bustling Rialto market and in the boats of floating greengrocers, these thistles are bought whole by the pile or the already peeled *fondi* (artichoke bottoms), and most often prepared very simply, sautéed in a bit of olive oil and wine and finished with lemon.

1¼ CUPS COLD WATER, PLUS MORE IF NEEDED

2 LEMONS

12 SMALL ARTICHOKES

4 TABLESPOONS EXTRA-VIRGIN OLIVE OIL

¼ CUP WHITE WINE

SALT, TO TASTE

2 TABLESPOONS CHOPPED PARSLEY

Add 1 cup water and the juice of 1 lemon to a large mixing bowl and set aside. Remove the dark green outer leaves of the artichokes, until you reach the inner pale green and yellow leaves. Peel the stalks and trim them to about 1 inch from the base. Cut the tops off and cut each artichoke into quarters. Immediately transfer to the lemon water to avoid browning.

Heat 3 tablespoons of the oil in a heavy-bottomed frying pan over medium-high heat until shimmering. Add the artichoke quarters and reduce the heat to medium, frying them until just golden brown, about 5 to 7 minutes. Add the wine and cook until it evaporates, about 5 minutes, and then add the remaining ¼ cup water, reduce the heat to low and cover. Allow the artichokes to cook for about 15 minutes, or until fork-tender. If the artichokes begin to dry out before they are tender, add more water. Transfer to a serving dish, drizzle with the remaining 1 tablespoon of oil and squeeze half of a lemon over the top. Season with salt to taste, and garnish with a pinch of chopped parsley. Serve with toothpicks to skewer.

SPIEDINI DI MARE

TERRONI, Los Angeles, CA • MAKES 6-8 skewers

Spiedino—the diminutive of *spiedo*, meaning "spit" or "skewer"—most often refers to a meatball that has been skewered and cooked. It's essentially the toothpick-lanced cocktail meatball of Italy. This summer-ready version reimagines the toothpick snack, Venetian style, where skewers and paper cones of fresh seafood, herbs, and citrus can be found at stalls lining the Rialto market each morning. Shrimp and octopus are readily available at most seafood counters, but squid, lobster, and thick cubes of fish would work in this recipe as well.

½ CUP BREAD CRUMBS

1 GARLIC CLOVE, FINELY CHOPPED

2 TABLESPOONS FINELY CHOPPED PARSLEY

1 TEASPOON SALT

WOODEN SKEWERS

½ POUND CHERRY TOMATOES

1 POUND LARGE PRAWNS, PEELED AND DEVEINED

1 POUND SQUID CHOPPED INTO 2-INCH PIECES

2 TABLESPOONS OLIVE OIL

LEMON WEDGES

In a small bowl, mix together the bread crumbs with garlic, parsley, and salt.

Assemble each skewer with a cherry tomato, a prawn, and a piece of squid. Repeat once more.

Sprinkle each skewer with the bread crumb mixture, and shake off any excess. Place on a plate in the refrigerator and let marinate for 30 to 45 minutes.

Prepare a grill to medium heat. Brush the skewers with olive oil. Place on the grill for about 2 minutes on each side, or until the prawns are pink and the squid is curled.

Alternatively, add olive oil to a cast iron frying pan over medium-high heat. Place skewers in the frying pan for about 2 minutes on each side, or until the prawns are pink and the squid is curled.

Serve with the lemon wedges.

CROSTINI

The folklore about crostini's origins holds that before there were individual serving dishes, there were slabs of bread that were often soaked in oil and other cooking liquids to help relieve staleness. When served at the table, they were heaped with whatever was for dinner, and used as a sort of edible plate. Consider the crostini a sort of archaic predecessor to the modern bread bowl.

These combinations are simply jumping-off points for making your own "little toasts." In Venice, *baccalà mantecato* (whipped cod) is a popular crostini topper, as are all means of artichokes, lagoon-grown vegetables, chicken livers, and any combination of meat and cheese. We were most inspired by the sea of toast options—that, en masse, appear rather like Italian sushi—presented at Al Timon, a canal-side bacaro that awakens right as the sun begins to descend.

FRESHLY BAKED, CRUSTY BREAD (LIKE BAGUETTE OR RUSTIC ITALIAN), SLICED CROSSWISE

EXTRA-VIRGIN OLIVE OIL

CROSTINI TOPPINGS (PAGES 146–151)

Brush the bread slices with the oil, and toast or grill over medium heat until golden. Spread crostini topping on the toasted bread, assemble on a platter, and serve.

SAGE AND WHITE BEANS

MAKES 1 cup

2 ½ TABLESPOON
EXTRA-VIRGIN
OLIVE OIL

6 SAGE LEAVES

1 CUP COOKED OR
CANNED WHITE
BEANS, DRAINED

1 SMALL CLOVE
GARLIC, FINELY
CHOPPED

ZEST OF HALF
A LEMON

SALT AND PEPPER,
TO TASTE

In a small saucepan over medium-high heat, heat
1 tablespoon of olive oil until shimmering. Using tongs,
place the sage leaves into the oil and fry for 5 seconds
on each side. Place on a paper towel-lined plate to drain.

In a separate bowl, add beans, garlic, lemon zest, and
1½ tablespoons of olive oil. Leave whole or mash the
beans into the oil until they make a rough paste. Add salt
and pepper to taste. To serve, spoon the mixture onto
toasted bread and top with a fried sage leaf.

HAZELNUT PESTO AND
ROASTED TOMATOES

MAKES about 1½ cups

¾ CUP HAZELNUTS

2 CUPS FRESH
BASIL LEAVES

½ CUP FRESH
PARSLEY

3 CLOVES GARLIC

1 TABLESPOON
SALT, PLUS MORE
TO TASTE

¾ CUP EXTRA-
VIRGIN OLIVE
OIL, PLUS MORE
FOR COATING
TOMATOES

¾ CUP PARMESAN

PEPPER, TO TASTE

ZEST OF 1 LEMON

2 CUPS CHERRY
TOMATOES

Heat the oven to 190°C. Place the hazelnuts on a
parchment paper-lined baking sheet. Roast for about
5 minutes, or until the nuts brown and the outer skin
starts to break. Remove from the oven and transfer to
a clean kitchen towel to cool. Roll the nuts up inside the
kitchen towel and roll them back and forth to loosen the
skins, removing any remaining skins by hand; set aside.

Add the hazelnuts, basil, parsley, and garlic to the bowl
of a food processor and pulse until well combined. While
the processor is running, add the ¾ cup of oil slowly,
working in batches if necessary, until smooth. Add the
parmesan and lemon zest, and blend. If the mixture is
too dry, add more olive oil until the texture is that of
a smooth and spreadable paste.

Increase the oven temperature to 230°C. Lightly coat
the tomatoes in oil and spread them evenly on the
parchment paper-lined baking sheet. Roast, tossing
at least once, until the tomatoes are blistered and
beginning to burst, about 20 minutes. Remove them
from the oven and let cool.

Spread each toast with a layer of pesto, top with two
tomatoes, and sprinkle with salt.

CHICKEN LIVER PÂTÉ

ANTHONY SASSO Casa Mono, New York City, NY
MAKES about 2 1/2 cups

2 TABLESPOONS EXTRA VIRGIN OLIVE OIL

1 SHALLOT, FINELY CHOPPED

2 CUPS CHICKEN LIVERS (SEE NOTE)

SALT, TO TASTE

4 SPRIGS THYME, LEAVES ONLY

1/2 CUP PEDRO XIMENEZ SHERRY

1 CUP DOUBLE CREAM

1/2 CUP CHICKEN STOCK

1 TABLESPOON HIGH-QUALITY BALSAMIC VINEGAR

ZEST OF 1 LEMON

In a low-sided pan over medium heat, warm the oil. Add the shallot and cook until soft, about 5 minutes. Add the livers (drained) and turn the heat to high. Season with salt and thyme leaves and cook for about 2 minutes.

Reduce the heat to medium and add the sherry. Deglaze the livers, allowing the liquid to reduce by half, about 4–5 minutes. Add the cream and chicken stock. Cook for about 5 minutes, or just until the livers are cooked through but not tough. Add the balsamic.

Using a ladle and working in batches, spoon the cooked livers into a blender with just enough cooking liquid to create a puree resembling the consistency of creamy peanut butter. Then pour into a very fine mesh sieve and push the meat with the back of the ladle until all of the juice is gone. Continue in batches until all of the livers are pureed and pressed. Discard any extra liquid. Season the livers with more salt and refrigerate for about 1 hour before using.

Spread each toast with a generous layer of chicken livers, top with lemon zest, and serve.

PREPARING CHICKEN LIVERS

Remove each lobe from the centre vein and place the livers in a bowl filled with milk for at least 1 hour before using. Sometimes the livers are sold pre-soaked in milk; this simply neutralizes some impurities.

RICOTTA, PROSCIUTTO, AND FRESH SEASONAL FRUIT

MAKES 6–8 crostini

½ CUP RICOTTA CHEESE

6 SLICES PROSCIUTTO

FIGS, STRAWBERRIES, OR OTHER SEASONAL FRUIT, SLICED

SALT AND PEPPER, TO TASTE

HIGH-QUALITY BALSAMIC VINEGAR (OPTIONAL)

Spread 1 tablespoon ricotta cheese on a piece of toast. Top with a slice of prosciutto and a slice of fruit. Season with salt and pepper to taste and drizzle the balsamic vinegar over the top.

BACCALÀ MANTECATO AND HOT RED PEPPER

MAKES 6–8 crostini

½ CUP BACCALÀ MANTECATO (PAGE 151)

1 TEASPOON DICED HOT CHERRY PEPPERS MARINATED IN OIL (SEE NOTE)

SALT AND PEPPER, TO TASTE

Spread 1 tablespoon of baccalà on a piece of toast. Top with a scant ⅛ teaspoon of hot peppers. Season with salt and pepper.

NOTE

Cento and Sclafani are the most widely available, but there are better Italian options at specialist shops and delis.

ROCKET, MOZZARELLA, AND CURED ANCHOVY

MAKES 6–8 crostini

½ CUP ROCKET

6 OUNCES FRESH
MOZZARELLA,
SLICED CROSSWISE

6 TO 8 CURED
WHITE ANCHOVIES

SALT AND PEPPER,
TO TASTE

Top each slice of toast with a few leaves of rocket, a slice of mozzarella, and 1 anchovy. Season with salt and pepper.

ARTICHOKES AND FRIED PANCETTA

MAKES 6–8 crostini

¼ CUP OLIVE OIL

6 TO 8 SLICES
PANCETTA

6 TO 8 SMALL
ARTICHOKES,
CLEANED, HALVED
AND SAUTÉED
(PAGE 141)

PEPPER, TO TASTE

In a large sauce pan over medium heat, warm the oil until shimmering. Add the pancetta (in batches if necessary) and sautée until crispy, about 5 minutes per side. Set aside to cool on a paper towel-lined plate.

Top each slice of toast with an artichoke and a slice of pancetta. Season with pepper.

BACCALÀ MANTECATO

MAKES 1¾–2 cups

The story of how Norwegian stockfish ended up as one of Venice's favourite ingredients begins with a fifteenth-century shipwreck and ends with the Venetians' love for all things aquatic. In 1431, when Venetian ship captain Pietro Querini and his crew were sailing for Bruges, they were shipwrecked in the Lofoten Islands of Norway. On that subpolar archipelago, Querini observed the local method of preserving cod by letting it dry in the wind on trellises, and then tenderizing it "with the back of knives until it becomes as thin as nerves." When returning to Venice, Querini brought the stockfish with him. The fish is still imported and made to this day into *baccalà mantecato*— a creamy spread served on polenta or toast. The word *baccalà* was adapted from the Portuguese word for salt cod, *bacalao*.

12 OUNCES DRIED STOCKFISH

½ CUP EXTRA-VIRGIN OLIVE OIL

SALT AND FRESHLY GROUND BLACK PEPPER, TO TASTE

Place the stockfish in a large pot with a lid, cover with water, and soak overnight. Bring the stockfish and the water to a boil over high heat, and boil for 10 minutes. Drain and break up the cod in a bowl, removing any bones. While the cod is still hot, begin whisking quickly while drizzling oil in slowly. Cod will begin to take on a whipped texture after much whisking. You may need more or less oil depending. Add salt and pepper, spread on the toast, and serve.

MONDEGHÍLÍ

INSPIRED BY Ratanà, Milan • SERVES 6–8

Most Americans know meatballs via the southern Italian tradition, filtered through decades of appropriation to combine some permutation of ground meat and red sauce. But in northern Italy, the meatball has an entirely different personality born of a peasant dish, or *piatto povero*, picked up from the sixteenth-century Spaniards that dominated Milan.

1 POUND VEAL OR BEEF SHANK

1 CARROT, PEELED AND ROUGHLY CHOPPED

1 MEDIUM ONION, ROUGHLY CHOPPED

1 CLOVE GARLIC, ROUGHLY CHOPPED

¼ CUP FINELY GRATED GRANA PADANO OR PARMIGIANO-REGGIANO

2 EGGS

1 PINCH NUTMEG

1 CUP TORN STALE BREAD, SOAKED IN ¼ CUP MILK FOR 10 MINUTES

SALT AND PEPPER, TO TASTE

1 CUP BREAD CRUMBS

¼ CUP OLIVE OIL, PLUS MORE IF NEEDED

Place the veal or beef shank in a large pot and cover with water. Bring to a low boil over medium heat, then reduce the heat to low and simmer, skimming any fat that rises to the top. Add the carrot, onion, and garlic. Keep at a low simmer and cook until fork-tender, 1½ to 2 hours.

Drain, reserving the broth for risotto or another dish. After the meat has cooled, shred by hand or with two forks, discarding any fat or bones. Add the shredded meat to a food processor with the cooked vegetables and pulse a few times to break up the mixture.

In a medium bowl, combine the meat mixture with the cheese, 1 egg, the nutmeg, and the soaked bread. Season with salt and pepper.

Roll the meat into balls slightly smaller than a golf ball. Whisk the remaining egg in a shallow dish. Place the bread crumbs in another shallow dish. Dip the meatballs into the whisked egg and coat in bread crumbs.

In a large frying pan over medium heat, warm the oil. In batches, fry the meatballs, turning to brown until golden on all sides. Place on a paper towel-lined plate to drain.

FONDI DI CARCIOFI

MAKES 8

In the Campo San Giacomo Rialto of Venice's San Polo neighbourhood is Osteria Bancogiro, a young establishment with a deceitfully ancient facade, where spritzes con Select (Venice's favourite red bitter) and half a dozen plates of crostini dot every counter and table. This recipe is an adaptation from one of Bancogiro's seasonal cicchetti options built from the broad, circular *fondi*, or bottoms, of artichokes, topped with creamy, fresh mascarpone cheese and a single oily anchovy.

3 CUPS COLD WATER

JUICE OF 1 LEMON

8 ARTICHOKES

2 TABLESPOONS EXTRA-VIRGIN OLIVE OIL

1 CLOVE GARLIC, FINELY CHOPPED

4 OUNCES MASCARPONE

8 CURED ANCHOVIES

SALT AND PEPPER, TO TASTE

Combine water with the lemon juice in a bowl. Cut the stem off of each artichoke, and using a sharp knife, peel away the outside layer of leaves in a circular motion. Cut off a thin slice at the base of each artichoke to remove the tough end, and then cut off a slice, half an inch thick—this is the artichoke bottom. Allow bottoms to soak in the lemon water until ready to cook to avoid browning.

Heat the oil in a saucepan over medium-high heat. Add the garlic. Remove the artichoke bottoms from the lemon water and pat dry. Place the artichoke bottoms in the pan and sauté quickly. Add enough water so the bottoms are covered and simmer for 15 minutes or until tender. Drain and dry.

While the artichoke bottoms are still warm, spread a layer of mascarpone cheese on each bottom, and top with an anchovy. Sprinkle with salt and pepper.

POLENTA

Polenta has been made in Italy since Roman times, when grain was coarsely milled and churned into porridge or hardened bread. Before it became an heirloom staple at Whole Foods, it was a functional food rather than a stylish one, rounding out the diets of Italian peasants. Across northern Italy, it's still made in copper pots via vigorous, continuous stirring, and often served as a sort of cornbread toast piled with baccalà or seafood in Venice, or sausage and onions in the Alto Adige. During Roman times, it was made with primitive grains like spelt and millet, morphing into the yellow or white corn variety when maize was brought back from the New World.

In this version, leftover minced meat and bread are soaked in milk and then combined with cheese and egg, rolled into balls, coated with breadcrumbs, and fried. This recipe comes from a restaurant in the Porta Garibaldi neighbourhood of Milan.

2 TABLESPOONS UNSALTED BUTTER, PLUS MORE, FOR GREASING

6 CUPS WATER

1 TABLESPOON SALT

2 CUPS YELLOW CORNMEAL (POLENTA GRAIN)

1 TABLESPOON OLIVE OIL (OPTIONAL)

TOPPINGS (PAGE 156)

Butter a large baking tray.

In a large pot, bring the water to a simmer and add the salt. Stir in the cornmeal a bit at a time, stirring with each addition. Stir continuously for the next 15 to 20 minutes or until the cornmeal reaches the consistency of thick pudding. Add the 2 tablespoons butter, stir, and spread the cornmeal onto the buttered sheet pan. Let cool and solidify, about 30 minutes.

Once the polenta has cooled, cut into small squares. Grill or quickly sear in a saucepan with the oil before composing polenta squares, if desired. Add either of the toppings on next page, then serve.

CONTINUED

LARDO-WRAPPED PRAWNS

MAKES 1 cup

1 TABLESPOON EXTRA-VIRGIN OLIVE OIL

8 LARGE PRAWNS, SHELLED AND DEVEINED

¼ POUND LARDO, VERY THINLY SHAVED INTO SMALL SQUARE SHEETS

1 TABLESPOON SPRING ONIONS, FINELY CHOPPED

In a small frying pan, over medium heat, warm the oil. Add the prawns and cook until just pink and curled, 2 to 3 minutes. Let cool.

Heat the grill. Wrap each prawn in a sheet of lardo. Top the polenta squares with wrapped prawns, and sprinkle with the spring onions. Place the composed polenta squares on a baking sheet and grill for 30 seconds or until the lardo melts over the prawns. Set aside to cool slightly, then serve.

SAUSAGE AND ONION

MAKES 1½ cups

2 TABLESPOONS EXTRA-VIRGIN OLIVE OIL

1 LARGE ONION, THINLY SLICED

SALT AND PEPPER, TO TASTE

½ POUND SWEET ITALIAN PORK SAUSAGE LINKS, COOKED AND THINLY SLICED

In a medium frying pan over medium heat, warm the oil. Add the onions and stir to coat with oil. Sprinkle with salt and pepper and stir occasionally until the onions are soft, translucent, and sweet, about 15 minutes. Remove from the heat and let cool.

Top each polenta square with 1 tablespoon of caramelized onions and 2 slices of the sausage, then serve.

ACKNOWLEDGMENTS

First, thank you to Ten Speed Press—especially Kelly and Aaron—for letting us write so many words on such a seemingly obscure topic. Thank you to our friends and photographers Dylan + Jeni for being the wonderful human beings that you are—and for bringing this book to life. Thank you Matthew Allen for your incredible patience and illustration skills. Thank you to our designer, Margaux Keres, for putting all the pieces together with grace.

To Tony Biancosino and Ashley Santoro, for stuffing yourselves into cars, trains, AirBnBs, and airplanes with us, drinking all the wine and spritzes with us, and generally making us better, more easygoing people.

To Alex Day, Natasha David, and Proprietors LLC, for the endless advice, the space, the recipes, the emergency pebble ice, the last-minute mint, and your constant generosity. You've saved our asses more than once.

To Katie Parla, for the guidance, the translation, the testing, and the generous amount of Italian knowledge you have shared with us, and the world. There's no one else we'd like to travel through Italy with more than you.

To Kathryn Bangs and the teams at Sydell Group and The Line Hotel. To Dan Sabo and the team at the Ace Hotel Downtown Los Angeles. To Jim Kearns, Hanna Lee, and the teams at Happiest Hour for letting us saber prosecco in your bar and squeeze citrus in your bathroom. And to Max Stefanelli and the Terroni team, thank you for letting us take over your kitchen, your bar, and your restaurant. Your enthusiasm and generosity was beyond anything we expected. And your Aperol Betty is tops.

To Elizabeth Colton, Vito Casoni and everyone at M Booth and Campari Gruppo. Thank you for your support and generosity.

To Fulvio Piccinino, who has been an invaluable resource and friend to us throughout this process. Your kindness and knowledge know no bounds.

And last but not least, thank you to all of the people who lent their shaking skills, brains, and/or elbow grease to this book: Roberto Bava, Greg Best, Dario Comini, Dom Costa, Rachel Erdman, Rachel Black, Roberto Pasini, Guido Zarri, Lucca Picchi, Nino Perrone, Alan Tardi, Leonardo Leuci, Giorgio Fadda, Jim Meehan, David Wondrich, Polpo London, Mario Piccinin, Eric Seed, Maurizio Stocchetto, Ingrid Williams, Anthony Sasso, and many more.

WHERE TO SPRITZ IN ITALY

MILAN

BAR BASSO • The bar where the Negroni Sbagliato was born, Bar Basso is the best place to observe the Milanese milieu from fashion designers to elderly sweater-vested men, all while drinking from a flower vase-sized, hand-cut glass.

BULGARI HOTEL • One of the many designer hotels peppered throughout Italy's capital of fashion, the stunning Bulgari Hotel is hidden behind a grove of lush gardens in a ritzy neighbourhood. Aperitivo here is simple, modern, and best enjoyed on the terrace.

CAMPARINO • Housed in the magnificent Galleria Vittorio Emanuele II, the Camparino bar is ground zero for Milan's original bitter liqueur, Campari. Here, the Milano-Torino can be had in its original glory.

CERESIO 7 • This scene-y rooftop pool and bar will require a reservation, but once in, it's a thoroughly entertaining affair. Avant-garde cocktails, excellent snacks, and spritzes flow at the flashy bar whose guests are equally gilded.

TURIN

BANCO VINI E ALIMENTI • This little market-café specializes in oddball wines and Italian beer, but the spritzes are made with Mauro Vergano's culty Americano aperitivo, and can be paired with exceptional charcuterie and cheese boards.

CAFFÉ MULASSANO • Supposedly the birthplace of the tramezzini sandwich, Caffé Mulassano presides in one of Turin's glittering 19th-century arcades and feels as if it's stuck—thankfully—in the city's first era of coffeehouses and vermouth drinkers.

VENICE

ALL' ARCO • This lunchtime-only spot is hidden on a side street underneath an old archway. Specializing in seafood-driven ciccheti, All' Arco dispenses everything from bacalà to langoustines alongside spritzes.

AL TIMON • Al Timon is one of Venice's greatest examples of the aperitivo tradition as experienced by locals. Tucked into the Canareggio neighbourhood, Al Timon is a cantina bursting at the seams with residents who line up to order crostini and spritzes by the dozen.

AL MERCA • Though it's most notable for natural wines, Al Merca captures the spritz life in its most modern incarnation. Nightly, crowds of young Venetians line up at this tiny counter for wine and spritzes, and then spread out onto the piazza.

CAFFÉ FLORIAN • This 18th-century café sprawling across St. Mark's Square maintains all its ancient charm, from the velvet booths to the suited waiters bearing trays of spritzes and snacks. Morning to midnight, it buzzes with locals and tourists alike seeking a bit of la dolce vita.

OSTERIA BANCOGIRO • An unassuming café-restaurant in Venice's Rialto neighbourhood, Bancogiro has a large patio and an excellent selection of cicchetti including traditional polenta and crostini topped with everything from seafood to fresh cheese.

BAR TIEPOLO AT THE WESTIN EUROPA & REGINA • Manned by longtime bartender Giorgio Fadda, this hotel den is a quiet respite for the international traveller seeking a bit of luxury away from Venice's tourist-filled streets. All of the Italian classics—spritzes to Negronis—can be found here, as well as enlightening conversation should Fadda be on hand.

PADUA

CAFFÉ PEDROCCHI • While it certainly isn't the cheapest place to grab a spritz in Padua, it's among the most famous. Expect plenty of marble, red velvet, and a solid aperitivo setup at this café that dates to 1831.

CORTE SCONTA • A tiny pocket square of a bacaro that is practically the opposite of Pedrocchi's gilded old-school scene. Young and buzzy, the tiny no-frills bar is packed to the gills nightly with locals spilling out onto the street from the tiny counter with plates of cichetti, spritzes in hand.

TREVISO

BOTEGON • One of the city's most beloved aperitivo bars, frequented by twentysomethings and octogenarians alike, particularly thanks to the excellent selection of traditional Trevisano cicchetti and fried foods.

TRIESTE

EPPINGER CAFFÉ • While this historic spot specializes in sweets, Eppinger turns into one of the most popular spots for a spritz and savory snacks come happy hour.

GRAN MALABAR • A tiny bar focused on Friulian wine (not surprisingly) and classic, no-frills *rebechin*, which are essentially Trieste's take on classic Venetian cicchetti.

SALUMARE • A sleek, modern "fish laboratory"—this tiny spot doles out rebechin featuring everything from smoked to spreadable fish alongside sparkling wines and, of course, spritz.

ÏNDEX

TRANSWORLD PUBLISHERS
61–63 Uxbridge Road, London W5 5SA
www.penguin.co.uk

Transworld is part of the Penguin Random House group of companies
whose addresses can be found at global.penguinrandomhouse.com

 Penguin
Random House
UK

First published in the United States by Ten Speed Press
an imprint of the Crown Publishing Group
a division of Penguin Random House LLC, New York

First published in Great Britain in 2017 by Bantam Press
an imprint of Transworld Publishers

Copyright © 2016 by Ten Speed Press, a division of
Penguin Random House LLC

Photographs copyright © 2016 Dylan + Jeni

Illustrations copyright © 2016 by Matthew Allen

Design by Margaux Keres

Talia Baiocchi and Leslie Pariseau have asserted their right under the
Copyright, Designs and Patents Act 1988 to be identified as the authors
of this work.

Every effort has been made to obtain the necessary permissions with
reference to copyright material, both illustrative and quoted. We
apologize for any omissions in this respect and will be pleased to make
the appropriate acknowledgements in any future edition.

A CIP catalogue record for this book
is available from the British Library.

ISBN 9780593079430

Typeset in 8/11pt Milano
Printed and bound in China by Toppan Leefung

Penguin Random House is committed to a sustainable
future for our business, our readers and our planet. This book
is made from Forest Stewardship Council® certified paper.

3 5 7 9 10 8 6 4 2